Praise for
Robots Make Bad Fundraisers

Steven's book hits on all cylinders when it comes to the best way to communicate with your donors. While there's a place for "robots" and automatic messaging or automated approaches, Steven gives you many examples of how robots can make mistakes and thus hurt your donor retention. So, keep a human eye on your "tools" and never waiver using your human intuition and touch. Your donors will love you for it and you'll keep them longer! And I'm grateful to Steven for taking the time to write this book, well done!

—Erica Waasdorp, President, A Direct Solution/Author
Monthly Giving. The Sleeping Giant.

Recently, I was talking about a back massager and when I opened my phone, I saw ads showing me the latest back massagers. Coincidence? Technology helps us accelerate the way we learn, the way we do business, and the way we give. But what happens when AI stands for "all in" in your fundraising operations? Steven challenges us to take our reliance on technology off autopilot, take the wheel, and shift gears into a more human centered approach to philanthropy.

—Kishshana Palmer, CFRE - Founder & CEO,
Kishshana & Co. + The Rooted Collaborative

Every professional fundraiser and/or volunteer involved with fundraising about to dive into this book will be so delighted they did. The cutting-edge insights and proven best practices begin early and literally keep jumping out of every page turned!

—Jay Love, The Fundraising Standard

I was trapped by the table of contents for Steven's book. Pay attention people! "Why retention eats acquisition for breakfast." Yes, yes, yes! Next, "The Dangers of Too Much Automation in Fundraising." Yippee! The internet and all that stuff is not the answer to all of life's challenges or opportunities. Can you imagine a tech company leader actually telling us fundraisers that technology is not the answer to everything?! How cool that is! Read this book...because robots really aren't good fundraisers!

—Simone P. Joyaux, ACFRE, Adv Dip, FAFP

ROBOTS
MAKE BAD
FUNDRAISERS

ROBOTS
MAKE BAD
FUNDRAISERS

How Nonprofits Can Maintain
the Heart in the Digital Age

STEVEN SHATTUCK

BOLD & BRIGHT
— M E D I A —

Published by Bold & Bright Media, LLC.
319 Becks Church Road
Lexington, North Carolina 27292
Boldandbrightmedia.com

ISBN-13: 978-0-578-65162-0

Library of Congress Control Number: 2020934188

Bold & Bright Media is a multimedia publishing company committed to bold hearts, bright minds, and storytellers whose experiences will inspire and compel others to grow in their own greatness. For more information visit BoldandBrightMedia.com.

"Anything that takes the human out of fundraising is bad."
—Simon Scriver

Contents

Introduction   1

Part I: The Case for the Personal Touch

Chapter 1: Why Retention Eats Acquisition for Breakfast   9

Chapter 2: What Research Tells Us Donors Want   13

Part II: Donor Management Software

Chapter 3: Data Collection and Management   23

Chapter 4: Data Segmentation   27

Chapter 5: Using Segments for Advanced Reporting and Communications   31

Chapter 6: Seglumping   41

Chapter 7: Data Stewardship   47

Chapter 8: The Dangers of Too Much Automation in Fundraising   53

Part III: Your Website and Online Giving

Chapter 9: Search Engine Optimization   65

Chapter 10: Online Giving – The $5 Experiments   73

Chapter 11: Pre-Donation – The Online Giving Page   77

Chapter 12: Pre-Donation – The Online Giving Form   83

Chapter 13: Post-Donation – The "Thank You" Page   89

Chapter 14: Post-Donation – The Automated Email   95

Chapter 15: Continuous Improvement Through
A/B Testing   105

Chapter 16: Peer-To-Peer   109

Part IV: Email Marketing

Chapter 17: When You Can and Can't Send
A Mass Email   119

Chapter 18: Email Deliverability and Spam Filters   125

Chapter 19: Email Scheduling   131

Chapter 20: Personalization and Merge Tags in
Mass Emails   135

Chapter 21: Why the Sender's Email Address Matters   141

Chapter 22: Making Your Email Newsletter Stand Out   145

Chapter 23: Turning Away Donors with Automated
Out-of-Office Emails   151

Part V: Social Media

Chapter 24: Digital Sharecropping in the
Social Media Age   159

Chapter 25: Examining the Facebook Algorithm   163

Chapter 26: The "Three A's" – a Winning Social
Media Content Strategy   167

Chapter 27: LinkedIn – The Undervalued
Secret Weapon   173

Chapter 28: The Art of Social Listening   177

Part VI: Giving Tuesday

Chapter 29: Preparing for and Standing Out
on Giving Tuesday   189

Chapter 30: Writing Email Subject Lines for
Giving Tuesday   193

Chapter 31: Giving Tuesday and Monthly Donors   195

Chapter 32: Giving Tuesday Follow-Up Segmentation   201

Part VII: Crystal Ball – Future Predictions and What to Look Out For

Chapter 33: A Multi-Channel Renaissance   209

Chapter 34: Gamification   215

Chapter 35: Augmented Reality and Virtual Reality   219

Chapter 36: Machine Learning/AI   221

Chapter 37: Favorite Tools, Vendors and Resources   223

Conclusion   227

References   231

Introduction

In some ways, we're in a golden age of fundraising. There have never been more ways to capture attention, rally supporters, generate revenue, and measure fundraising performance than there are today. The accessibility of this technology has also never been greater, even to the smallest charities.

When the robots work, amazing things can happen. We can A/B test the performance of emails and donation forms, stream high-definition video from the other side of the globe with a device that fits in our pocket, dissect website traffic data down to single visitor behavior, and predict donor behavior, thanks to artificial intelligence and machine learning.

And yet, for the past 40 years, philanthropy as a percentage of total GDP in the United States has stubbornly remained at 2%, according to Giving USA. Meanwhile, average donor retention rates haven't budged from the mid-40% in the nearly two decades that they've been studied by the Fundraising Effectiveness Project.

In their special report "The Disappearing Donor," *The Chronicle of Philanthropy* reports that from 2000 to 2014, the share of Americans donating to charity fell from 66.2% to 55.5%. According to Giving USA, giving in 2018 declined by 1.7% when adjusting for inflation. Employee burnout is the rule, not the exception, with the average tenure of a fundraiser lasting just 18 months.

With all of the software, tools, apps and intelligence available to us, why has fundraising performance stagnated? Sure, overall charitable giving is on the rise, but that's mostly due to stock market performance and the participation of mega-wealthy donors. Why is this happening? Why were 20th- and even 19th-century fundraisers, without all these tools, able to raise just as much money as their 21st century counterparts? The truth is that we've lost touch with what makes fundraisers the most successful: **a personal connection with our supporters.**

It's easier to fire off an email newsletter to our entire list than it is to pick up the phone to say thanks to a donor. It's easier to post a Facebook update than it is to write a handwritten note. The experience of donors on our websites is more transactional than transformational. Our donor databases are messier than an attic. We flood mailboxes with incorrectly addressed letters. We shake our fists at the algorithms that keep our mediocre content from newsfeeds. We agonize over Giving Tuesday and the annual golf tournament. We treat our donors like identical ATMs and wonder why they stop giving. We succumb to the "cult of free" during system selection. We let the finance or membership department choose the fundraising software that makes their lives easier, rather than what enables high donor lifetime values. Automation is our highest ideal.

We've all had bad experiences with for-profits caused by an over-reliance on technology. More and more our daily lives are mediated by algorithms. We no longer need to talk to a human to order and consume basic services. For this to become the norm in the nonprofit sector—a sector built on relationships—would spell doom.

That's not to say that digital tools should be avoided by fundraisers. Quite the contrary; but technology should support us, not replace us. It should be invisible, not a shiny object or a silver bullet. The factory approach to fundraising is hurting the sector, but it doesn't have to be this way. We don't have to leave it to the robots. Technology works best when it enables relationship-building, instead of taking its place. The email newsletter isn't the evolution of a print newsletter; it's a companion. A.I. shouldn't replace the prospect researcher; it should aid them. A handwritten note can follow a tweet. An auto-generated email receipt can put a smile on a donor's face.

Adding one or more layers of technology rarely seems like a bad idea. After all, vendors are quick to tout the benefits (reduced costs, reduced staff time, ease of use, better data collection, etc.). But for cause-based organizations, where personal connections and relationships are paramount, technology can sometimes get in the way. A donor can have an equally bad experience on an online donation page or be addressed as "|FNAME|" in an email instead of by their actual name. Inaccurate wealth screening data can lead to incorrect assumptions, data breaches can erode trust, and vendor outages can turn off potential donors.

Nonprofits also have numerous opportunities to purchase technology solutions that promise to solve relatively minor or non-existent problems. You can replace a paper auction bid sheet and an ink pen with a tablet, but what happens when the donor isn't familiar or comfortable with the interface of that device? Or if the network connecting the devices goes down? You can set up a point-of-sale device that swipes credit cards at an event, but if that's your only payment option and a donor would feel better writing a check, what then? You can download a font that looks like human handwriting, but spend more time trying to line up the envelope in your printer tray than it would have taken to write it out yourself. Even the biggest for-profit companies still haven't quite perfected this technological renaissance we live in: *"Dear @Amazon, Yes, I recently bought a humidifier. No, that doesn't mean I'm in the market for lots more humidifiers. In fact, it means that I won't need another humidifier for a good number of years. Thanks for reminding me that the AI apocalypse is a long way off." - @Yascha_Mounk*

Hopefully, you aren't picturing me as an old man, yelling at neighborhood kids to stay off his lawn.

I'm not saying that technology should be avoided or feared. I'm saying that we should apply time-tested principles of philanthropy to the modern technology available to us as fundraisers—with the goal of keeping the donors we already have, inspiring new donors to give, and maintaining the sanity of our team members.

In this book, we'll do just that.

If at any point while reading this book you'd like to see a video, an email, a social media post, research, or anything else I reference, be sure to visit https://robotsmakebadfundraisers.com.

Part I

THE CASE FOR THE PERSONAL TOUCH

Our modern-day lives are filled with instant, impersonal transactions.

Without interacting with a single human or even leaving your couch, you can perform most of your daily routine tasks—as well as the advanced ones, like buying a car, furnishing a bedroom, or applying for a loan.

Even post-sale interactions are mostly automated. Online chat has almost completely replaced the customer service phone call. This has led to a dehumanization of brand interactions. Few transactions end with a smile or a handshake, and we only have conversations when something has gone wrong.

While a few brands stand out, it's likely that few customer service experiences will stay positive as more of our daily activities move online.

But there's one sector that should be immune, one that should rise above all the others and always surprise and delight its constituents—regardless of the communication channel—the nonprofit sector.

Unfortunately, many charities have fallen into the trap of letting the robots take over—letting too many communications become automated, transactional and impersonal. While automation has lowered the cost and difficulty of new donor acquisition, it has arguably had an equally negative impact on existing donor retention.

In this first section, I'll make the case for a focus on retaining the donors you already have. And I'll back up those claims with research into what donors want and expect from the organizations they support. Then, we'll spend the rest of the book applying those principles to digital channels that so often lack the human touch that encourages philanthropic support.

Let's dive in!

CHAPTER 1

Why Retention
Eats Acquisition for Breakfast

When I bought my first house in 2007, there was an empty flower bed in the front lawn. I went to a nursery and spent about $250 on plants and supplies. When I got home, I filled the bed with new, vibrant plants.

For a couple weeks, they looked great, but ultimately, I neglected them. I didn't water them, prune them, fertilize, pull weeds, etc. Everything wilted eventually, and I had to go back and spend another $250 to gain back that curb appeal.

This time I took care of them, and it cost very little in comparison to replacing the plants (just a little water and my time). Now, years later, they bloom every spring and look great (as long as I'm diligent in my care).

Gardening is not dissimilar to fundraising.

After you convince a donor to make their first gift, do you cultivate that relationship through simple, personalized communications, or, do you let the relationship wilt, only to have to replace the donor entirely?

If you're anything like the average nonprofit, it's the latter.

In 2006, the Association of Fundraising Professionals (AFP) and the Center on Nonprofits and Philanthropy at the Urban Institute established the Fundraising Effectiveness Project (FEP) to conduct research on fundraising effectiveness, with a particular focus on donor retention.

FEP's crown jewel is their annual Fundraising Effectiveness Survey Report, which consists of an analysis of data collected from thousands of participating nonprofits. Thanks to the cooperation and support of the members of the AFP Donor Software Work-group, which includes companies like Bloomerang, Neon, and DonorPerfect to name a few, anonymized data flows from these software vendors to FEP, resulting in a comprehensive report on the gains and losses of the participating nonprofits.

Since 2006, the report has grown to include billions of dollars in transactions, thus offering a robust snapshot of the sector overall. While each report is rich in data, followers typically anticipate the FEP reports for one key metric: the average donor retention rate, or the percentage of donors who give from one year to the next.

In the nearly two decades since the study began, donor retention hasn't fluctuated much outside of the 40th-45th percentile in any year analyzed, much like the stubborn 2% of GDP. Suffice it to say, if you're reading this book in 2020 or later, you can bet that the current average donor retention rate is somewhere in the low-to-mid 40s.

In other words, the sector on average loses more than half of the donors who gave in the previous year. This somewhat alarmingly low rate is a main contributor to why fundraisers find themselves with the difficult task of achieving financial sustainability through a major gift and planned giving pipeline.

According to Adrian Sargeant, one of the world's foremost authorities on donor loyalty and engagement, "we're caught on this treadmill where we have to spend lots of money on acquisition, which most nonprofits lose money on anyway, just to stand still."

The news is worse for first-time donors (those who have only given one gift), where retention rates are around 20%, and dropping:

- 2014: 24.3%
- 2015: 25.1%
- 2016: 22.5%
- 2017: 22.4%
- 2018: 20.2%

In other words, more than two-thirds of first-time donors never give again.

The good news is that for repeat donors (donors who have given at least two gifts), retention rates hover around 62%, meaning that if you can get a second gift your odds of building a long-term relationship are greatly improved.

Why Retention Trumps Acquisition

Maybe you're thinking, "Okay, so what if donors don't give in consecutive years? They might come back someday."

Think again.

According to FEP, the recapture rate for lapsed donors is an astonishing 4%, and has been on the decline for the last five years:

- 2014: 6.45%
- 2015: 5.76%
- 2016: 5.01%
- 2017: 4.57%
- 2018: 4.00%

If donors stop giving, there is a very small chance that they will ever give again.

It's also a more expensive process than keeping the donors you already have. According to James M. Greenfeld's book *Fund Raising: Evaluating and Managing the Fund Development Process*, new donor acquisition via direct mail can cost between $1 and $1.25 per dollar raised, while donor renewal costs are only about 20 cents per dollar raised.

Finally, keeping donors longer can produce revenue beyond your current line of sight.

The late, great Jerry Panas found that those most likely to leave you a bequest (a gift in their will, with gift amounts averaging around $32,000 here in the U.S.), are not the wealthy. They are, in fact, those that have been giving to your nonprofit previously for five years or more, and especially those that have been making monthly donations or multiple gifts within a year.

So how can we improve these low retention rates and keep donors longer? Let's look at what academic research tells us.

CHAPTER 2

What Research Tells Us Donors Want

There is a mountain of research into what motivates (or doesn't motivate) donors to continue to support nonprofit organizations.

Yes, philanthropy is deeply personal, and much like trying to map poetry a la Dead Poets Society, it's hard to quantify and define the psychology behind altruistic motivations in a way that applies to every situation, every organization, and every individual.

But we do have enough information to at least get us started down the path.

Why Donors Leave

For his 2001 study "Managing Donor Defection," Adrian Sargeant surveyed the lapsed donors of 10 national nonprofits and asked them one simple question: Why did you stop giving?

These were the answers that were given:

- 5% – thought charity did not need them
- 8% – no info on how monies were used
- 9% – no memory of supporting
- 13% – never got thanked for donating
- 16% – death
- 18% – poor service or communication
- 36% – others more deserving
- 54% – could no longer afford

Aside from death and financial difficulties, these reasons for lapsing are almost entirely preventable. It all boils down to the quality of communications, specifically reporting on program outcomes and output, and thanking the donors.

Interestingly, the reasons for why donors stay loyal tend to mirror the ones given for why they stop their support.

Why Donors Stay

In 2011, DonorVoice collaborated with around 250 nonprofits to find out what they had done well to keep about 1,200 donors loyal for many years. A survey was sent to those loyal donors with a list of 32 things that nonprofits do well for their donors. The survey asked recipients to rank items that mattered the most to them and by order of importance.

Here are the top seven:

1. Donor perceives your organization to be effective in trying to achieve its mission.
2. Donor knows what to expect from your organization with each interaction.
3. Donor receives a timely thank-you.
4. Donor receives opportunities to make their views known.

5. Donor is given the feeling that they are part of an important cause.

6. Donor feels their involvement is appreciated.

7. Donor receives information showing who is being helped.

These top seven items that mattered to loyal donors almost directly correlate to the findings of Dr. Sargeant in a survey that was administered 10 years prior and from a completely different data set. Again, the items that mattered are just as controllable.

In his 2011 book *Building Donor Loyalty: The Fundraiser's Guide to Increasing Lifetime Value*, written with Elaine Jay, Sargeant defines his "7 Principles of Donor Loyalty." They are:

1. Ensure your "customer service" is good.

2. Reinforce shared beliefs.

3. They're aware of consequences.

4. Connect with them.

5. They trust you.

6. There are multiple engagements.

7. They're learning. Are you taking them on a journey?

If these were the biggest donor loyalty factors from 2001-2011, a relatively low-tech era compared to today, my fear is that the situation has been, and will continue to be exacerbated by the ubiquity of impersonal, automated processes and communications.

If these factors are not convincing, one only needs to look at the excellent annual donor surveys of Penelope Burk and Cygnus Research. Year after year, her interviews with donors corroborate decades-old research. Inside, you'll find quotes like:

"There were two instances this year where I made gifts over and above what I had intended, and they both involved personal contact from someone in the development office (director or gifts officer). Being thanked for my previous gift was much more persuasive than receiving multiple emails and direct mail letters."

McConkey-Johnston International, which is out of the United Kingdom, also found that first-time donors who get a personal thank-you within 48 hours are four times more likely to give a second gift.

The strategies for retaining donors are simple, but that's not to say they're easy. Often it takes a large shift in the mindset of a nonprofit organization to begin focusing on retaining donors rather than just simply acquiring them.

Donors want to know how their dollars are being used, that you appreciate them and value their opinions, that you consider them as the real change agents (as opposed to your organization), and that the communications you send them are crafted just for them.

This means that if the technology you're using doesn't help you retain donors, it's harmful.

Nurturing a donor relationship isn't easy, but it is simple in practice. And technology can be just as helpful as it can be harmful.

Now that we know why retention matters, what donors want from us, and how the personal touch can help, let's look at a few places where technology enters into the conversation, and how it can aid us rather than impede us.

We'll focus on a few main areas:

- Donor management software
- Your website and online giving
- Email marketing
- Social media

In each section, we'll cover how you can use these tools to give donors what they want. We'll also cover how algorithms and automation come into play, and how you can optimize them to your benefit.

Finally, we'll wrap up with some advice and examples on how to weave these channels together, as well as some recommendations for further reading and tools you should consider using.

But first, a quick disclaimer.

Before embarking on optimizing your use of any of these tools or worrying about implementing new tech, know that they should come further down a list of prioritizations. All too often I see fund-raisers on online forums and Facebook groups clamoring for advice on how they can implement text-to-give, acquire Google ad grants, or get their hands on some other shiny object. In only the rarest of instances can any one piece of technology be a silver bullet for your fundraising or donor retention efforts. If it were as easy as waving a magic wand, our sector would have much higher retention rates.

At the risk of undervaluing this book, there are many, many things that should take priority over digital, not the least of which includes:

- strong board governance and engagement, including term limits and 100% board giving
- documented job descriptions
- a documented strategic plan
- a documented development plan, including donor steward-ship strategies
- a documented diversity, inclusion, and equity policy
- a documented succession plan
- a documented marketing and communications plan, including a crisis communications plan
- a documented gift acceptance policy

- a gift agreement template, including a morality clause
- a rubric for measuring program or mission impact
- documented organizational priorities and challenges

If you do not have most of these items in place, please pump the breaks on your digital efforts. It is unlikely that such items could be implemented successfully without an organizational culture that is conducive to success.

Many of the items will not take long to create. That being said, let's dive into leveraging technology in a useful and responsible way.

Part II

DONOR MANAGEMENT SOFTWARE

Along with your website, your computer, and your phone, your donor management software or donor database is on the short-list of vital assets.

Having records of who your supporters are and their past interactions is the first step in getting them to give again.

Donor databases have come a long way from filing cabinets full of index cards, three-ring binders, and Excel spreadsheets. Like Google, donor databases now come equipped with algorithms that can parse your donor data in useful ways. They can also be used to automate many of your previously manual processes, like letter and email generation, reporting, and task/appointment scheduling.

While most are powerful, donor databases often go under-utilized—a shame for an asset with such potential, not to mention costs in annual fees.

So often we as fundraisers and nonprofit communicators are at the mercy of tech giants, like Google and Facebook. However, your donor database is just waiting to serve you. It will give you the greatest ability to implement the research previously discussed and deliver the communications that donors want.

So, let's look at some vendor-agnostic strategies for making the most out of your donor management software, concentrating on four key categories: data collection and management, reporting and segmenting, data stewardship, and automation.

CHAPTER 3

Data Collection and Management

Clear, concise data entry policies and procedures are critical to enabling you to create useful segments. After all, you can't run a donor report by constituent type if information is not consistent. You can't filter a report by a city if you've entered the full name of the city in one record (San Francisco) and an abbreviated version in another record (SFO). And if multiple staff members are entering data into the database, it's likely that the format of your data will be all over the map.

Documented and accessible data entry policies and procedures also protect you from staff turnover. Imagine if your database is managed by only one team member, and that team member were to suddenly leave the organization. Without a policy document, not only would you not know how things were done, but you can be sure that things would be done a different way by the next person, resulting in even messier data.

One of the best things is to create a *Donor Management Software Data Policies and Procedures* document. It's a living document to which your database users can refer when entering and recording data. It should cover how data is recorded onto constituent profiles, how transaction data is recorded, and how to create and access reports in a standardized way.

A quick Google search for "sample donor management software data policies and procedures" or "donor management software data policies and procedures template" will get you a document from which to get started.

Once you have a policy for how data is inputted, you can now turn your attention to what data should be collected.

Deciding What Data to Collect

You're likely already tracking basic contact and demographic information for each constituent in your database. But a database really becomes powerful when you customize constituent profiles with additional information that is meaningful to your organization or that reflects your supporter's alignment with the cause. For example, an animal shelter may want to know its constituent's favorite breed of dog, while an advocacy organization may want to track what congressional district each of its constituents live in. The World Wildlife Fund asks new members what areas of conservation they are most interested in and how they participate in conservancy.

One question that is not only relevant to all organizations but is also infinitely powerful and actionable is, "Why do you donate?" Knowing the difference between a donor who had a grandparent who died of the disease you're trying to eradicate versus someone who saw a Facebook ad and compulsively donated will allow you to communicate to those constituents in very different ways.

All this is not to say that you should load up your forms with tons of questions about the donor. Phone calls, in-person visits and tours, events, and donor surveys are excellent ways to gather information about the donor after they've donated. Whatever you decide, make it a priority based on what you will actually do with the data.

Speaking of what you will actually do, let's look at some tangible ways to put this data to work for you.

CHAPTER 4

Data Segmentation

How you leverage your donor database has one of the greatest impacts on your overall retention rate. One of the most popular metaphors for low donor retention rates is a leaky bucket. And with good reason. We spend a lot of time and effort acquiring new donors, only for more than half of them to never give again. We're caught in an endless cycle of refilling the bucket as best we can.

The more I thought about this ubiquitous metaphor, the more I realized how ironic and self-fulling it truly is.

The primary reason we have a leaky bucket is because we are putting all of our constituents into one bucket in the first place.

Regardless of who they are, why they gave, how often they give and what they give, they all go into the same bucket—our donor database.

Once they're in the bucket, we are sending:

- the same newsletter to everyone
- the same appeal to everyone
- the same thank-you letter to everyone
- the same event invitations to everyone

Is it any wonder that the bucket starts to leak?

To make things worse, all of those unengaged donors who haven't given in a few years because they moved away, or they passed away get pushed further and further toward the bottom of the bucket. Even if we wanted to hear from them, we wouldn't be able to.

When we treat our donor database as one giant bucket of names, it becomes impossible to deliver personalized and contextualized communications.

Would you send the same birthday message to all your friends, coworkers and relatives, including your mother? Of course not. Each message would have a format and content tailor-made for that one recipient. You would tell your mother you love her, and how much she means to you. You wouldn't give your boss the same risqué greeting card as your bestie.

With one bucket, we send out an appeal to someone who passed away last year (only for a surviving relative to receive it).

With one bucket, we send a physically demanding volunteer appeal to someone with mobility issues.

With one bucket, we invite an out-of-town donor to a local event.

With one bucket, we send an email newsletter that covers every imaginable topic but fails to resonate with any one recipient.

Think of it this way:

Imagine the last time you were driving and merged onto the highway from an on-ramp.

Did the traffic pattern change just for you? Of course not. You had to adjust your speed and lane preference to everyone who was already on the interstate. It's not a fun exercise.

Even though we as motorists have accepted this reality, donors do not take the same experience so lightly.

Take, for example, first-time donors. They make their first donation and get thrown into an already in-progress campaign— whatever communications schedule our nonprofit already has up and running—no matter who they are, what they donated, or why they donated. First-time donors may get an appeal before they are even thanked for their first gift because an email was already scheduled to be sent. Feeling disengaged, recipients ignore your communications, and eventually they leak out. After all, who wants to be put in a bucket? A bucket which is gross, made of cheap plastic or rusty iron, and diminishes donors down into a storable commodity?

Instead of this robotic, one-size-fits-all approach to donor management, what we need is to treat our donor databases as a collection of buckets, custom-tailored to the types of constituents with whom we are trying to communicate. When this happens, the communications can then be tailored for maximum impact.

This practice is generally referred to as donor data segmentation. A segment is simply a small group of constituents who share the same attributes, such as "first-time donors," "out-of-town donors," "donors who give less than $100 a year," or "monthly donors" just to name a few. Segments typically start off as reports in your database, which then become email or direct mail distribution lists.

Unfortunately, segmentation is not yet a ubiquitous practice among database managers and fundraisers. Back in 2014, I teamed up with my friends at Nonprofit Marketing Guide to see how nonprofits were (if at all) segmenting their online and offline communications. Four hundred twenty-five respondents, most with budgets less than $5 million, responded to our survey. We found that a little over 80% were familiar with the term "communication segmenting" but only a little over 60% were actually segmenting their email newsletter or direct mail lists. Of those who were segmenting, donation amount and previous interaction history were the most common methods used for segmentation. Of those who weren't segmenting, a lack of knowledge on how to do it, and mistrust of their data were most commonly cited as the reasons why they weren't.

Like most things, bad segmentation is worse than no segmentation. It's better to send out the same thank-you letter to everyone than send a customized thank-you letter to the wrong recipient. Our segments are only as good as the data we proactively collect and regularly cleanse. But it doesn't have to be a chore.

Speaking of chores, let's talk about reporting! Just kidding, it will be fun, I promise.

CHAPTER 5

Using Segments for Advanced Reporting and Communications

When you see the phrase "donor data segmentation" do you start envisioning a team of 100 super nerds crunching out complex formulas on expensive software? Banish that thought! You can do segmenting yourself no matter what type of software you're using (though it may be a tad harder if you're using Excel rather than a dedicated donor database).

No super nerds required!

In fact, donor data segmentation is nothing more than a form of reporting, and you probably run reports all the time.

The difference here is that we're going to be proactive, rather than reactive. Running a report like a LYBUNT (last year but unfortunately not this year) or SYBUNT (some year but unfortunately not this year) only tells us what has already happened with our donors. We are going to run reports that will enable us to make something we want to happen actually happen!

The most common segments include:

- **Recency:** How long have they been giving?
- **Frequency:** How often are they giving?
- **Type:** How are they giving?
- **Amount:** How much are they giving?
- **Reason**: Why are they giving?
- **Interest:** What topics are they most interested in?

In practice, these segments will appear as reports in your database like "first-time donors," "monthly donors," "donors who have given for more than 5 years," or "volunteers who have never donated."

Acknowledgments, appeals, and stewardship pieces should look different for all of these segments. For example, an appeal to a monthly donor should say different things than an appeal to a volunteer who has not yet donated. Not wildly different, mind you, but different enough that the constituent type is contextualized. There is no limit to the amount of donor communications segments you can create, and the more you do create, the more personalized they will be.

Now that you have your segments, you can stop sending the same gift acknowledgment, appeal, or newsletters to every single person in your donor database. Not only will the messaging be tailored for each recipient, the timing of those messages will be appropriate for them. Remember our highway metaphor? Each donor is going to have a personal, private lane, and will receive appeals, invitations, and stewardship pieces only when it makes sense to receive them.

Never again will you have to worry about a new donor receiving an appeal for a gift just days after donating because you already had a campaign queued for everyone in your donor database. Never again will you have to worry about accidentally asking for an insultingly low gift amount from a potential major gift donor. Donor data segmentation will empower you to transition from a spray-and-pray communicator to a strategic donor love champion! Remember: according to DonorVoice research, the second highest reason why donors stay loyal is that they "know what to expect from your organization with each interaction." Setting this expectation is virtually impossible if you are not segmenting your donor data.

While there is an almost infinite number of ways to segment or to organize your donors into smaller groups, consider these seven segments as easy ways to get started.

1. First-Time Donors

As we mentioned before, these donors are at the greatest risk of lapsing. But, again, they're not all alike. You can further segment them by dollar amount—perhaps, over $100 and below $100. A first-time donor who donates less than $100 has an average retention of 18%—lower than the average rate of 23%. Retention increases as the size of the gift increases, but even at $250 or more, it's still less than 50% retention.

So why focus on first-time donors at all? There's a great reason. If you can encourage the first-time donor to give again, retention rates rise significantly. For amounts of $250 or more, the repeat donor retention rate is more than 75%. The key is to treat them special. After they donate, thank them quickly, ideally within 48 hours. Remember that study from Adrian Sargeant: Donors want to be acknowledged quickly. Make a great first impression of how you will treat them. In that thank-you message, explain how the gift will be used. Send a welcome package. If possible, invite them for a tour of your location or out for a cup of coffee. Do what makes sense to you. For larger gifts, you may want to be more creative. Consider a survey about their interests, a handwritten thank-you note, a phone call. Just something to make them feel special.

Focusing on first-time donors is a good place to start. They have the lowest retention rates and the highest acquisition cost. Create a documented communications plan for them, and only them. In other words, first-time donors only get what is on this plan and nothing else, regardless of whatever campaigns you're planning or already have in progress.

No matter when donors give, they only receive these communications in the first year. If they give in October, they don't receive your holiday appeal! If they give in March, they don't get your spring appeal! They're not ready for it.

You can create a plan like this for any donor type, and even create multiple variations based on gift size or reasons for giving.

2. Monthly Donors

If you have donors who have basically said, "Hey, you can go ahead and charge the card every month," circle those people. They're super special. According to a Target Analytics study, retention rates among monthly donors reached as high as 78% in some sectors.

Think of it this way: You have an opportunity to send them up to 12 thank-you messages rather than just one. Be creative. Outline the awesome things you did with funds each month. Or send unusual, fun holiday cards—National Salad Month for May or Admit You're Happy Month in August.

Set up a report to see which credit cards are expiring in two months. Send a special note before the expiration date. Remind them of all the great things you've been able to accomplish together. Don't treat the donor like an ATM by simply saying, "We need your new credit card number."

3. Lapsed Donors

It's impossible to achieve a 100% donor retention rate. Some donors may only intend to make a one-time gift. Some may move away and lose touch, while others may go through financial hardships. Assuming your donors are human, they will eventually die someday!

You should neither get too hung up on lapsed donors, nor write them off completely.

Begin first by isolating donors who haven't given in two years. Data from the Fundraising Effectiveness Project shows that once a donor has lapsed, there is only about a 4% chance that they will ever give again.

From here, separate them into sub-categories:
- Were they memorial or tribute donors?
- Were they peer-to-peer donors?
- Did they give to you for many years consecutively and then suddenly stop?
- Did they only give to you once?

You can and should take very different, proactive approaches to each of these.

Memorial donors may have only wanted or expected to have a one-time engagement with you, likely because they were supporting their friend, the bereaved. Peer-to-peer donors may have not fully understood what organization their gift went to, likely because they were supporting their friend, the fundraiser. In the future, consider having that third party introduce you to the donor as an organization that is worthy of long-term support.

Consider sending a survey to the other sub-segments to find out why they stopped giving, and then to see if you could actually bring them back into the fold. The survey could give you more information about how to communicate with other donors. You may not get many responses, but there's a possibility of converting some of them into repeat donors.

It could also be that the donor has passed away. A data service known as deceased suppression processing notifies you if someone in your donor database has passed away. Use it as an opportunity to reach out to a surviving relative to express thanks for the legacy of their loved one.

Other lapsed donors may have simply moved away. Consider an NCOA (National Change of Address) data service to compare your mailing addresses with the USPS (United States Postal Service) database. Those lapsed donors may still like you, but simply lost touch because they moved!

4. Volunteers Who Have Never Donated

It's possible that you may have current active volunteers who have never made a cash donation. This is an easy one. Consider this segment as low-hanging fruit because volunteers are ten times more likely to donate than non-volunteers, according to a study by Fidelity Charitable.

Don't be afraid to ask for a donation. If you ask in a way that makes sense and appeals to donors' interests in your cause, you're likely to be successful in encouraging them to donate—even though they're already donating their time.

5. Donors Who Have Shared Feedback–
Positive or Negative

Not only should you welcome criticism, you should encourage it. A survey by Target Analytics found that donors who complained are retained at higher rates than those who don't complain. Complaining is a strong signal that these donors care about your organization and its future.

Send a survey to all of your donors, including first-time donors, every year. In addition to finding out more about them ("Why did you first give?" "What's your connection to this cause?"), you should encourage them to give honest feedback by posing questions like "What are we doing right?" "What are we doing wrong?" and "What do you expect out of us?"

Those who respond, whether positively or negatively, are signaling to you that they are engaged. Even if you only get a few responses, this type of feedback will be invaluable in guiding your relationship-building efforts with the donor.

6. Social Media Followers
Who Interact with You

When it comes to identifying small groups of your most engaged donors, it's hard to do much better than those who follow you and interact with you on social media. Not only have they opted in (followed you) to receive your posts and tweets, the channel itself is a great way for personal, one-on-one interactions that you can't get through other channels.

Having a donor database that listens for mentions on social media, records those interactions on a constituent's profile, and stores their usernames and profile URLs on their profiles will be indispensable in building this segment.

But it's not enough to just wait for these interactions to come to you. You should often highlight these supporters on social media yourself. Tag donors and volunteers (or invite them to tag themselves in the case of Facebook) to say thank you for their support. When tagged, the posts will show up on all of their individual profiles. It's a great way to steward supporters and to promote your charity.

Having built this segment, you are able to leverage these loyal supporters during digital campaigns such as Giving Tuesday or other online days of giving. Consider mobilizing digital campaigns, to use social media to make and to share your content, or to come to your own defense should someone say negative things about you on social media.

7. Long-Term Donors

If you're treating your long-term donors the same as you do all of your donors, you're long overdue for a change. For example, if your loyal donors are receiving the same correspondence as new donors, which outlines how you're using funds, you are likely annoying them. It is information they have already heard before.

However, you should never underestimate the power of the right message. Donors would be interested in a recent example of a person or family whose life has been impacted. You could also go into more details about new initiatives, seeking valued input.

Roll out the red carpet for these donors. Give them the royal treatment. Always think of donors as partners who have truly invested in your organization. You'll find natural ways to communicate with them with the right mindset.

Sending personalized communications is essential to building donor relationships that last. The alternative is throwing all of the donors into one bucket and hoping that they do not leak out. (Spoiler: They will.)

In the next chapter, we will look at an example of how lumping everyone into one bucket can be bad, even if you have the best intentions.

CHAPTER 6

Seglumping

The other day I received a donation appeal that contained a curious sentence.

It read:

"Whether you donated today, previously have given, or still plan to give, we thank you for your ongoing support in our mission."

I had seen it before, this practice of listing all the possible reasons for sending a communications piece to all the possible recipients.

That same day, the preeminent Beth Ann Locke, director of advancement at Simon Fraser University, bemoaned a similar acknowledgment she received.

It read:

"We know you just bought tickets or made a donation, or maybe you just subscribed, so we want to send you a big THANK YOU!"

Instantly, we became obsessed with not only getting to the root cause of this practice, but also naming it. After workshopping several ideas, Beth Ann came up with a winner.

Allow me to introduce a new term to the nonprofit lexicon: Seglumping.

Seglumping is that act of referencing multiple audiences in one unsegmented communications piece.

Lumping + Segments = Seglumping.

To be fair, seglumping is almost always done with the best intentions, usually as an attempt at inclusiveness, or as a result of not having the tools required for proper segmentation. It's a holdover from mass media communications (radio, TV, etc.) where audience segmentation is impossible.

It's also easy to rationalize the alternative.

Back to Beth Ann who asks us to imagine a fundraiser saying:

"We could segment the database . . . you know, so all the dog lovers get the doggy emails, and the horse people get the horse emails" and their boss saying *"Oh yeah? How is that gonna work? Because we haven't done it yet. Everyone likes getting all the animal emails. They are ANIMAL lovers!"*

One sign that you might be seglumping is if your letter or email contains a sentence that begins with "Whether you're a ...."

For example:

- Whether you're a long-time donor or haven't made your first gift
- Whether you've volunteered before or want to get started
- Whether you're passionate about the rainforests or the arctic
- Whether you've contributed to this campaign or you want to make an impact for the first time

There is no way that the rest of the content of your letter or email can be simultaneously compelling to both audiences. But more importantly, you risk alienating your loyal supporters.

In fact, my hierarchy would be

- Segmentation: Good
- No Segmentation: Neutral, at best
- Seglumping: Bad
- Bad Segmentation: Worst

Unfortunately, seglumping can alienate recipients when it hits their personal inbox, because it can be a direct slap in the face, rather than simply ineffectual. Yes, seglumping is actually worse than not segmenting.

The best segmented communications should not allow recipients to feel part of audience groups that they actually do not belong to. Instead, any of your best segmented communications should leave donors with subliminal feelings, as if they were the only donors that mattered to your organization. They should feel that your communications were written just for them and no one else. They are known. They are beautiful and unique snowflakes.

Conversely, seglumping shows recipients that they are just tiny fish in a big, crowded pond. It shows recipients that either you did not take the time, or you were unable to craft a message just for them.

Let's go back to my original example:

"Whether you donated today, previously have given, or still plan to give, we thank you for your ongoing support in our mission."

Let's say you're a monthly donor of $100 to an organization, having given for the past five years. You are being *seglumped* in with people who have never given or with those who (for some reason) are still being thanked for their "ongoing support."

43

Is it any wonder that in loyalty studies, poor communication is often cited by donors as a top reason why donations lapse?

An Exception: "Crossed Paths"

The one instance where it's not only acceptable, but recommended, that you reference in one piece multiple "potential" audiences is in multi-touch campaign letters, expected to span an extended period of time (weeks or more).

For example, let's say you're sending out three letters over a period of six weeks. Consider adding a line to the second or third letter that reads "If your donation and this letter crossed paths in the mail, we thank you!"

Here the donor won't be put off by the fact that they recently donated to a campaign for which they are also receiving an appeal.

The best possible thing that you can do is segment out those who have already contributed. But this is not always possible with drop dates, shipping times (to and from your organization), data entry, etc. Also, donors may possibly use a reply device that is not tied to the current campaign, or they may make an online donation instead of mailing a check, resulting in you attributing or designating the gift differently. With emails and online donations, there is less of an excuse for "crossed paths," especially if you have an integrated solution (database/email marketing/ online giving).

For example, if it's a special online day of giving and you're sending out multiple emails, consider adding, "If you've already made your donation today, we thank you!"

The first step toward change is awareness. Hopefully, this has made you aware that you might be seglumping. If you cannot segment, then don't seglump to compensate. If you can segment, then by all means, please do so. Your donors will appreciate it.

Now that you're a master donor data wrangler, let's talk about how to keep that donor data clean and useful over the long term.

CHAPTER 7

Data Stewardship

In the time since you started reading this book, some of the data in your donor management software has become outdated. At least one constituent has changed an email address, gotten a new job, moved to another state, donated to another nonprofit, changed banks, or perhaps even passed away.

As complex, time-consuming, and expensive the task of updating your donor data is, consider also the cost of not doing so, especially within the context of the following outcomes:

- Donors who change addresses
- Donors who pass away

Let's look at both individually.

Donors Who Change Addresses

At least 40 million Americans move each year. This is 17% of the U.S. adult population. What this means for a database of 15,000 accounts is that potentially 2,500 constituents may have different addresses within a year. This results in a significant cost to the organization as a result of delayed and returned mail.

The answer to this problem is an NCOA. What is an NCOA? The NCOA (National Change of Address) will update your mailing addresses. The updates include both the standardization of address formats per recommendations from the U.S. Postal Service and comparisons of addresses on file in the databases of the USPS and NCOA. Such updates also include data for all change of address requests, filed by U.S. postal customers within the past 48 months.

NCOA does not just find movers; it also documents correct addresses. If, for instance, *street, avenue, or road,* are missing from an address, corrections are made in the database. If directions such as *N, E, S, W, or NE* are missing from an address, corrections are made in the database. If a secondary address, such as apartment or suite number is missing or invalidated, corrections are made in the database. Also corrected are misspellings and "+4" is added to zip codes. Finally, the address format is corrected according to USPS standards.

There are times when a person has moved but the new address cannot be obtained. What this could mean is that a post office box has been closed with no forwarding address, people have moved to a foreign country, or people have moved and failed to provide a new address. Even though a new address cannot be provided, the NCOA database does help you to discover who may need follow-up or who may need to be removed from your mailing list.

Having all of your addresses up to date also helps facilitate duplicate checking. The reduced postage cost alone more than justifies the cost of an NCOA, not to mention the potential of higher return on investment (ROI) on your direct mail pieces, now that they're actually being delivered. If you claim preferred mailing rates, USPS requires that your mailing list be run through NCOA processing within 90 days of the mailing.

Next, let's review an unfortunate reality.

Donors Who Pass Away

Remember, according to Adrian Sargeant's research, 16% of donors lapsed because they died. When you combine that with the fact that a majority of charitable giving comes from older donors, running a data service known as a "deceased suppression process" regularly becomes invaluable.

In deceased suppression processing, the names and addresses of individual donors in your database are matched against public records of deceased individuals. If found, this allows organizations to identify deceased constituents and to mark them as such in the databases.

The cost of such a data service typically starts around $500; it is well worth the investment. Here are three reasons why.

1. Not Annoying a Surviving Family Member

Hopefully you've never experienced the loss of a loved one or close friend. In certain contexts, being reminded of them can bring up fond memories. Receiving direct mail addressed to them is not one of those contexts, especially if the content includes language like "Act now!"

Removing deceased individuals from your mailing list can save you the embarrassment of appearing insensitive to a surviving spouse or a household member. It is highly doubtful that individuals will notify your organization of relatives on your mailing list who have passed away (if they do, skip down to #3). Actually, it is unfair to have such an expectation.

You owe it to deceased individuals who have supported you not to cause an ounce of pain to their surviving loved ones. This alone is enough reason, but if you are not yet convinced, then read on.

2. Cost Savings

Let's imagine you invest $500 in a data service. At four mailings per year, with a cost of $0.49 per mailing, you would only need to remove about 250 names to fully justify the (hard) cost expense—especially if you have a large and old list that has never been cleansed.

Do not allow your desire "to break completely even" on the hard costs of data service keep you from investing in data service. Not annoying even a few donors is worthwhile.

3. Final Opportunity
to Show Appreciation (and More)

Learning that a dedicated and engaged donor has passed away should trigger a lot of activity for you as a fundraiser, especially if you have data on members of their households.

For example, sharing your condolences with a surviving family member is an amazing stewardship opportunity. In addition, make time to let a surviving family member know just how much you appreciated the support of the deceased donor. Share tangible outcomes. There is no greater act of appreciation than communicating the known and unknown legacy of a deceased donor.

Who knows? That spouse, partner, son, or daughter may continue supporting you in honor of the dearly departed.

Along with other data services like NCOAs, deceased suppression processing is an indispensable part of the fundraiser's toolkit. It's not hard to find a provider for such data services. It's likely that your current donor database provider can point you in the right direction, if not provide it directly.

Before we close out the donor management section of this book, I want to leave you with a word of caution. Our donor database is an amazingly powerful tool, but it can't completely do our jobs for us.

Next, let's look at some of the pitfalls of relying too much on our donor management software.

CHAPTER 8

The Dangers of Too Much Automation in Fundraising

We may yet reach a point when our donor management software can automate every single menial task that currently bogs down fundraisers.

Someday, our software will be able to take a donation, segment the constituent, and send a thank-you letter in the mail. Even now, technology exists that suggests which donor is ready for an upgrade ask or which donor might lapse in the next 90 days.

However, until the point when artificial intelligence can totally mimic humans, donor management software will not fully take the place of a fundraiser (and by the time robots finally take over completely, we will all probably perish).

Of course, just like segmentation, bad automation is worse than no automation. So, don't look to your software to totally replace you just yet. Let me tell you a little story that might have you thinking twice about setting up too many automated processes, especially given the personal nature of philanthropy.

As a millennial employed by a tech company, I was required by law to purchase and use a standing desk.

A few other Bloomerang employees purchased specific adjustable desks that allowed them to sit or stand. Seeing for myself how satisfied my co-workers were, I ordered the same kind of adjustable desk on the first day of September.

What happened between then and Halloween should be a cautionary tale for anyone interested in totally automating their customer or donor communications processes.

After making the purchase, I received an automatic email receipt that was rather perfunctory and bland—a topic we will cover later in the book.

Knowing that the adjustable desk would not arrive for a few weeks due to its high demand, I more or less forgot about the order.

That is, until I received an email appeal from Autonomous around the end of September, promoting their office chair.

Keep in mind that I had bought a *standing* desk, albeit an adjustable one.

You could argue that the timing of this email appeal was a little odd, especially since I was already a customer and I had not yet received my desk.

What made them think that I had the confidence to invest in a second chair? What made them think that I had personally used one of their products?

Those questions aside, it was the next email—received on the same day as the chair appeal—that made the situation truly interesting:

Hello Steven,

We want to thank you for your order. Unfortunately, there was a delay in production with the manufacturing of our desks that affects your estimated shipping time. The new shipping time frame for your order is Oct 20 - Oct 27. We are working hard to get your order fulfilled and on its way to you so that you can begin working smarter!

We apologize for the wait and appreciate your patience.

Just hours after sending me an appeal, they let me know that the shipping on my desk had been delayed a few more weeks. The shipping delay by itself probably wouldn't have annoyed me at all, but the fact that I had just received an appeal from them got me curious about how they decide who and when to send promotional emails to.

I was also struck by the desk company's sending email address: human@company.com. (We'll also talk more about these kinds of email addresses later on in this book.)

I decided to have a little fun with the desk company by replying. Can you guess what kind of reply I received? Do you think the following response came from a human?

##- Please type your reply above this line -##
We're working on your request (35076). We will be in touch soon. To add additional comments, reply to this email.

That struck me as pretty robotic and not at all human.

Luckily, later that day, a real person did eventually respond:

Hello,

I am very sorry about the delay on your order. Let me know if you have any questions and I would be more than happy to help you in any way i [sic] can.

Thank You,

Kaitlin H.

Customer Experience Rep.

After a slight stumble, the desk company did eventually come through with some pretty good customer service. I wasn't really mad to begin with, and I definitely felt better after getting the personal response. They even asked me to rate the support I had received.

But the story isn't over, dear friends. Remember, it was a full month before I received the desk.

Within this time span, I received more emails: seven emails to be exact, six of which were appeals for that same chair!

That's six appeals to a potentially still disgruntled first-time buyer who had not yet received their order. Six appeals for a product that is somewhat useless without said order.

Ironically, the appeals slowed down significantly after I received the desk (arguably the best time to start appealing to me). Just one email (an appeal) arrived in the subsequent 30 days.

So, what's the point of this standing desk rant?

The desk company likely fell into a trap that many organizations do when it comes to technology: They got sold on a system that promised improved processes and lower costs—thanks to automation.

I got subscribed the moment I became a customer to an already-planned or in-progress mass email campaign, regardless of my customer type or demographic. Most importantly, I was kept on that email marketing cadence regardless of the fact that my customer type changed (i.e. my order had been delayed; I had expressed negative feedback, etc.).

An automated system requires complicated sets of rules and exceptions that can move constituents to different segments and cadences. Robust systems like Marketo and HubSpot require hours of training to keep users out of trouble.

In addition, automation cannot quite account for donor motivations. This is why things like an automated welcome series for new donors should be approached with extreme caution. Unless all of your donors have the exact same motivation for giving, or you collect diverse sets of information when a gift is made, and your automation can segment accordingly, it's likely that you will be shooting blind with the content you send next.

In other words, how can you know that your automated, one-size-fits-all communications will hit the mark if you haven't yet gotten to know new donors?

If you get stars in your eyes over the promises of a fully automated system, understand no robot is going to do all of the work for you. At some level, your involvement will always be required.

Part III

YOUR WEBSITE AND ONLINE GIVING

My wife and I were recently searching for a new home church. After visiting one congregation for several weeks in a row, a friendly pastor introduced himself and invited us to attend an upcoming "new members" class planned for the following week. He told us the time and the place, and we said we'd be there.

A few days later, we got a very friendly and welcoming email from another pastor at the church (we had filled out an information card) with another invitation (and link to register) to the upcoming class. I clicked the link in the email, but I couldn't register because the webpage said registration for the upcoming class had already closed.

I wrote back: "Looks like registration is closed on that webpage, but please count us in if it's not too late. We have a 7-year-old and a 2-month-old." (I mentioned the latter because the registration page mentioned that childcare was available).

He replied: "Sorry about that. I didn't realize registration had closed. We will host another class in November, and we would love to have you join us for that one!"

Slightly annoyed but otherwise undeterred, I began the registration process for the next month's class.

The online form was pretty typical. I was asked for basic contact information and prompted to answer a couple of questions such as, "How did you hear about us?" and "Do you have any dietary restrictions?"

Next, I needed to add other members of our household to the profile. Adding my wife was simple, but adding the children was not. Because of how the form was built, it copied over the same fields from the section I filled out for myself, meaning I had to re-enter our home address for both children, as well as a phone number (neither our infant nor seven-year-old have a phone, so I re-entered my cell). There was one unique field in the child section: a drop-down with multiple options for age range: pre-school, primary, junior high, or high school.

Missing from the child section was a choice for infants.

Concerned that there might not be infant childcare at the church, and in lieu of no better option, we chose preschool for an infant, and then we proceeded to spend the next few weeks worrying about our selection.

As it turns out, an unexpected appointment took me out of town on the date of the class we registered for, and we asked if we could come the following month.

"We're not having a class next month, but we can register you for the month after that!"

So, four months after getting a nice, personal invitation (which we accepted), we finally made it to the class.

In defense of the church, I can understand why an online registration system is appealing. With such a system, the church can know exactly who is coming; it can plan for childcare, meals, staff needed, etc. Equally, the church can receive electronically the contact information of all of its attendees. Assuming that registration is a good experience, prospective attendees can register themselves, and on their own time. Attendees might even find their way to their classes via the website—and without a personal invitation.

For a church, few things are more coveted than a new, visiting family. Looking back, our accepting the church's invitation should have been the end. But rather than striking while the iron is hot, technology can become a barrier (to be fair, perhaps a week's notice was not enough time to accommodate an increased class size, but I wonder if the prospect of a new family joining a congregation should have outweighed the inconvenience?).

There are many ways in which issues manifest for donor-supported organizations. First and foremost is online giving.

Online giving is one of the fastest growing segments of philanthropic activity.

The Blackbaud Institute for Philanthropic Impact's *Charitable Giving Report: How Nonprofit Fundraising Performed in 2017* found that online giving in the United States increased 12.1% in 2017, while overall giving was up 4.1%.

However, online giving isn't the juggernaut that it sometimes seems to be. According to the same report, online donations accounted for just 7.6% of total fundraising revenue, up from 7.2% in 2016.

Other studies show higher growth. For example, the M+R 2018 Benchmark Study showed that online giving increased 23% in 2017, after 15% growth in 2016.

Regardless of the study that you choose to cite, there is no reason to suspect that online giving will do anything but continue to grow, as more and more of our daily activities move online.

Underscored is the need to make sure that online giving experiences are frictionless and rewarding for donors. Just because a one-on-one human interaction is not involved does not mean that fundraisers can't apply time-tested principles of philanthropy to the channel.

Unfortunately, time-tested principles rarely shine through in online giving. It is perhaps the prime example of what happens when the robots are left in charge.

But before we get to the advice on how to generate more online donations through an improved website visitor experience, we need to first generate website visitors.

CHAPTER 9

Search Engine Optimization

Recently a family of raccoons had to be removed from the attic of my in-laws' lake house.

When we asked the owner of the pest control company how he was able to remove them so quickly, his reply was succinct, funny, and purely logical.

He simply replied, "I think like a raccoon!"

Not only does that make total sense, but it's the best and most future-proof SEO strategy you can have.

What is SEO?

SEO, or search engine optimization, is the practice of modifying your website so that you appear in search results for the terms that are important to you.

If you wanted to appear in the search results for "animal shelters Indianapolis," the strategies and tactics you'd employ to do so would be considered SEO activities.

When it comes to SEO, concentrating on optimizing for Google is the best way to be successful.

Why? Because even though there are many search engines, the vast majority of searches are done through Google. And if you make Google happy, chances are you'll be optimized for other search engines as well.

Google represents the granddaddy of all robots that you are beholden to. Its algorithm (the secret formula that decides who shows up for what searches) is an ever-changing and closely held secret. Thousands of SEO consultants and agencies spend every waking hour trying to optimize and often manipulate their websites to ensure their employers and clients appear as high as possible in as many searches as possible.

SEO is somewhat less important for nonprofits, especially for the fundraisers of nonprofits, than it is for for-profit businesses. SEO is usually more important for your nonprofit's programs and services.

For example, it's unlikely that a donor would open up Google and search for "animal shelter Indianapolis" because they're looking to donate money to an animal shelter. What they're likely doing is looking to adopt a pet or perhaps even volunteer.

Were a prospective donor to use Google in order to facilitate a donation, it is likely that they've already made up their mind to do so (because your marketing has reached them some other way), and they simply need help getting to the donation page. In other words, they would search for your brand name "People for Puppies Indianapolis," find your website, and hopefully complete the donation.

That being said, it's important to look at SEO from both perspectives:

- Terms that describe your programs and services
- Terms associated with your brand or your brand name itself

Searching for "Google SEO Ranking Factors 20xx" will net you the latest thoughts on what works and what doesn't. SearchMetrics is one of my favorite sources for this information. Like donor psychology, the core philosophy around ranking factors does not change, though some minor shifts in the importance of each factor may fluctuate from year to year.

At the time of publication, the current most significant ranking factors are as follows:

- Page Speed – does your website load quickly, even on mobile devices?
- Security – does your website begin with https:// instead of just http:// (do you have an SSL certificate)?
- Mobile Friendliness – is your website responsive?
- Optimized Content – do the keywords and phrases you want to appear in searches also appear on your website, including your location and brand name?
- Technical SEO – do you have things like page title tags, meta descriptions, H1s?
- User Experience – do users spend a lot of time on your website, visiting multiple pages?
- Backlinks – do other reputable websites link to yours?
- Social Signals – are Facebook and Twitter users posting status updates that include links to your website?

Recently, Google shifted away from links and content (the things that were easy to game) to a greater emphasis on user experience signals. When it comes to user experience, responsive web design is likely the most important consideration. It's a mobile world, after all, and Google cares whether your visitors have a good experience browsing your website on a mobile phone.

For nonprofits, having a good mobile experience goes beyond how Google feels about it. Potential donors need to be able to find what they're looking for on your website and fill out your donation forms from any device. Not only could you get higher rankings on Google, but you'll definitely get more revenue.

What does not work when attempting to improve your search engine rankings are things like stuffing your page title tags, meta descriptions, or on-page content with keywords; building as many links as possible to your site no matter who it is that's linking to you; and publishing as many random webpages as possible just to increase the size and content depth of your website.

Many SEO service providers have literally gone out of business because their business models were based on either what Google once valued or on trying to shortcut what they currently value.

So, what are nonprofits to do?

Other than using a dedicated website and a content management system (Squarespace, WordPress, Firespring, etc.), or perhaps even engaging with an SEO consultant who further optimizes your website from a technical perspective (use this section of the book as a way to test their mettle), there are two main ways that nonprofits should catch the eye of Google while providing a useful service to their website visitors: owned media and earned media.

Owned Media: Frequent Blogging

Blogging has become absolutely indispensable to the SEO conversation, especially for nonprofits.

Frequently adding new blog posts to your website increases your site's word count and thus increases the opportunity for that content to appear in other search results—craft useful, relevant, educational and/or entertaining content. The more that new blog posts get read and shared, the higher your website's value is to Google.

Don't just talk about yourself. It's fine to blog about your recent fundraising event or to send an email about a new volunteer, but if your communications start and end with only what is going on in your world, it's unlikely that you'll create real engagement. What would happen, instead, if you published expert content that your community could view as a resource?

Find out what people want to know . . . and answer their questions! If your organization supports a specific cause, there are likely a lot of questions about that cause or issue that you could answer. For example, a quick search on Quora for "Alzheimer's caregiving" returns dozens of questions. These are potential blog, seminar, webinar, and newsletter topics that you could tackle to create value for not just your current constituents, but prospective ones as well.

Harness your internal experts. If you are worried about who will write all of this expert content, look no further than those within your organization. Your employees, volunteers, and board members likely have some expertise around the cause you support so harness this knowledge! The more authors you have contributing, the more expert content you can publish.

As your nonprofit starts to create expert content, your organization can evolve from "just another cause to support" into becoming a true resource in the community. Give it a try and see what happens!

Earned Media: Publication Relationships

A backlink is a link from another website that points to yours. Link building has been the bread and butter of SEO for as long as search engines have existed. You want other people to link to your website.

However, low-quality links can hurt you, so strive for a low quantity of high-quality links. For example, it's better to have one link from a major publication or media outlet than 50 from random directories.

That's exactly what earned media does.

To put it simply, earned media is getting someone else to talk about your organization. Paid media is advertising, and owned media is your website, blog, social media channels, etc. Earned media is getting someone else to talk about you, like a newspaper, blog, or other media outlet.

Building relationships with journalists and bloggers, as well as crafting relevant and compelling press releases, are the key steps toward a successful earned media strategy. Again, working with a dedicated public relations professional is probably your best course of action. Don't be afraid to bring on a PR student as an intern to concentrate specifically on this; there should be plenty for them to do!

Look at it this way: SEO isn't something you do, but the result of doing other things well. Once you have your website in technical order, owned and earned media will pay dividends beyond higher search engine rankings.

Know that SEO is a long-term play. There are few things you can do that will generate an immediate change in rankings. Like planting a tree, the best time to get started was yesterday. The next best time is today.

Search Engine Marketing (SEM), Paid Search, and Google Ad Grants

What we have covered so far is typically referred to as "Organic Search" but there is another side to the SEO game that deserves attention: "Paid Search."

Paid Search, often referred to as Search Engine Marketing or SEM, comprises the search results that you can pay Google directly to display. These are typically the first few results on any SERP (Search Engine Results Page) and are noted by an "Ad" icon.

As with any marketing effort, a paid search campaign requires knowledge and experience to be successful. Given that there will be little competition for your brand name (assuming there aren't other organizations who have the same exact name as you) it's unlikely that SEM will be a worthwhile investment for the average local nonprofit organization.

However, the fact that many organizations offer "ad grants" to give nonprofits a jumpstart on their SEM campaigns merits some discussion on the topic.

As I said, running a paid search campaign on Google is complicated. Frequently required is a large monthly budget to make sure that the ads generate views and clicks. Because of this, Google Ad Grants have always rubbed me the wrong way.

For one, Ad Grants are usually a drop in the bucket. A $10,000 ad grant will only get you a few days' worth of competitive ads, or a couple months of uncompetitive ads. In the business world, it's not uncommon to budget that much per week and have the campaign running constantly.

Secondly, ad campaigns require a lot of time and expertise to set up. Keyword research, audience targeting, copywriting, and where the ads point to (not to mention optimizing those landing pages) all need to be considered. The "free puppy" analogy is apt here.

Businesses will invest thousands of dollars into optimizing these campaigns, all before paying Google a dime to run them. It's not uncommon to find one or several marketers solely dedicated to paid search within a marketing department. These paid search marketers are constantly honing their craft, experimenting, testing, and tweaking. Their expertise is highly sought after, and their earnings reflect that.

This isn't meant to discourage you or condescend. With time and dedication, anyone can learn this craft. My point is that fretting over these campaigns (and seeking out the grants in the first place) distracts from higher-ROI activities, like donor stewardship.

With organic search, you can make pretty good progress on your own, but in the paid search realm, you'll hit a wall pretty quickly without help. At the same time, it is a skill worth investing in to develop, so if it sounds fun to you, go for it!

Now that we have a baseline for attracting more website visitors, it's time to talk about how to optimize their experiences on site, both before and after the donation is made.

CHAPTER 10

Online Giving – The $5 Experiments

For the past several years I've conducted "secret shopping" experiments where I picked a city in the U.S. and donated $5 to 50 of its nonprofits, chosen at random. I tracked the experience of donating and how each of the nonprofits interacted with me afterward.

All of the donations are made online through their websites directly. I used my real name, real address, real phone number, and real email address.

Each donation constituted a first-time donation to that organization. In other words, I was a new entry into their database.

My only other rule was that I had to fill out any questions on the form that they asked. If they asked for a phone number, they got one, even if it wasn't required.

The results of these experiments showed that when it comes to online giving, robots (websites, donor databases, and payment processors) are the primary communicators to donors, not humans. And I believe this largely accounts for why retention rates for online donors are significantly lower than those who give offline.

In the year I chose Indianapolis nonprofits, this is what I experienced:

Ninety-six percent sent an email receipt within 60 seconds of the donation as their first response.

- 22 of 48 emails were from the payment processor.
- 26 of 48 emails were branded from the organization.
- 5 of 22 organizations who sent payment processor emails also sent a branded email acknowledgment shortly after.

Four percent sent no acknowledgment of any kind. None made thank-you phone calls, despite 19 requiring a phone number.

Thirty-four percent sent a physical acknowledgment letter through the mail as the **second response.**

- The fastest letter came within 5 days of the gift.
- The slowest letter came within 13 days of the gift.

Twenty percent sent an email as the **second response.**

- 5 of 10 came on the same day as the donation.
- 1 of 10 came 1 day after donation.
- 2 of 10 came 3 days after donation.
- 2 of 10 came 13 days after donation.

Chicago's 50 donations had similar results.

- 45 organizations sent an automatic email first.
- 14 sent a thank-you letter by mail, 10 of which included a handwritten signature.
- Only one organization sent a new donor survey.
- Two sent a handwritten note by mail.

- None made a thank-you phone call.
- Two did not acknowledge the gift in any way.

When I chose Omaha as my victim, I increased the donation amount to $10 (again with the same rules and methodology as the previous experiments). My thought was that perhaps stewardship would improve if I increased my donation (Spoiler: It didn't, and I don't think giving $100 would have made a difference).

The Omaha results:

- 1 of 50 made a phone call
- None sent handwritten notes
- 2 of 50 did not acknowledge the gift
- 16 of 18 hand-signed their snail mail thank-yous
- 2 of 50 included an appeal in their first snail mail thank-you letter (a "thask")

It should be no surprise that Target Analytics found that retention rates for online gifts were typically 10% less than their offline counterparts.

In many ways, these $5 experiments were what led me to write this book. We treat online donors terribly, and it extends to social media followers and email subscribers.

If we want to improve the online giving experience, we need to look at a few elements of the process step-by-step:

Pre-Donation

- The online giving page
- The online giving form

Post-Donation

- The post-donation confirmation page
- The post-donation automatic confirmation email

Let's follow the donor journey and start with what happens on your website, pre-donation.

CHAPTER 11

Pre-Donation –
The Online Giving Page

For my $5 experiments, I also examined the makeup of the donation page and form, in addition to the post-donation communication experience.

In the case of Chicago, the 50 donation forms looked like this:

- Forty percent required a phone number. (This should be 0%, since a donor won't/can't donate if they don't want to give their phone number.)
- Eighty-two percent had a recurring gift option. (This should be 100%.)
- Eighty-two percent had giving level options. (This should be 100%.)
- Twenty-eight percent gave a choice of funds. (This should be 100%, or at least give the donor an idea of how the suggested amounts will be used.)

For Omaha, I expanded to look at the page, as well as the form:

- Sixteen percent had a clean URL, like "www.nonprofit.org/donate." (This should be 100% for sharing and confidence purposes.)
- Thirty-eight percent had a non-native donation form. (This should be 0% for confidence purposes.)
- Eighty-eight percent had an SSL certificate. (This should be 100% for security purposes.)

If these 100 organizations are any indication, we as a sector have a lot of optimization work to do. In this chapter, I'll explain why.

Getting a prospective donor to your donation page is only half the battle. So many things can happen on this page that will spell the difference between a lost donation and a lifetime giver.

Here are a few elements of a winning online donation page:

Website Native

Ideally, your donation form should live on a page that lives on your website. For example: charity.org/donate. When you redirect visitors from your website to a third-party site (like PayPal or Google Checkout), some trust may be lost.

Unlike a third-party online donation page, you are not sending a potential donor off-site to a page generated or hosted by your payment processor (like PayPal), a donor database, or a third-party online giving platform (like Network for Good).

Here is an example of both:

- **Website Native**
  - https://www.artsforlifenc.org/donate/

- **Third Party**
    - https://www.kintera.org/site/c.7oJILSPwFfJSG/
      b.8649985/k.8414/Donate_to_AJC/apps/ka/sd/
      donorcustom.asp?msource=ChicagoEMA

In the first example, you can see that the URL is very short, clean, and easy to say. If you were to visit this organization's homepage (artsforlifenc.org) and click the donate button, you'd be sent to https://www.artsforlifenc.org/donate/ and be presented with a form to fill out. You never leave the website, and it's a very natural experience for the prospective donor.

In the second example, you have a URL that is long, nonsensical, and is an extension of the online giving vendor's website, not the nonprofit's website. As a potential donor, you would go from "nonprofit.org" and click the donate button only to be sent to:

https://www.kintera.org/site/c.7oJILSPwFfJSG/
b.8649985/k.8414/Donate_to_AJC/apps/ka/sd/
donorcustom.asp?msource=ChicagoEMA

Another way to describe these types of pages is "on-site" vs. "off-site," or "embedded" vs. "redirected."

Ideally, the page may be designed to look a lot like the nonprofit's website but is hosted off-site. In most cases, however, this kind of donation page does not retain the design elements of the original nonprofit's website. Add that to the change in URL (from "nonprofit.org" to "kintera.org/site/c.70..."), and you run the risk of confusing the donor. Plus, you could never put a URL that long on a printed piece and expect people to type it in themselves.

Responsive

Given how much the Google algorithm favors websites that are mobile device-optimized, it's absolutely critical that your entire website be responsive. As more and more donors pledge their support via mobile devices, your donation page and form must function on all device types.

Reduced Navigation

A donation page should give the donor no pathways to navigate away from the page. Once they are there, you only want them to do one thing: Donate. Don't distract them with links to other pages. Don't make it easy for them to abandon the form. Instead, make it easy for them to fill out the form.

Supporting Content

Your donation page should include some supporting text, since it may be the first page of your website they see. You don't have to wait until after they've donated to thank them. Shower them with praise, let them know how much their donation will mean to those you serve, and make them the hero of the story. Photos that show the impact of their donations are also good but avoid videos since they can distract from filling out the form.

For technical trustworthiness, consider including a badge from your payment processor, database provider, or a third-party like GuideStar or PCI (showing compliance).

Privacy Policy / Statement

A link to your privacy policy should be pervasive throughout your entire website, and definitely accessible on your donation page. This policy simply states how donor information will be stored, used, and (not) shared. A simple Google search for "sample privacy policy" will net you some templates from which you can build your own.

SSL Certificate

An SSL (Secure Sockets Layer) Certificate transforms the http in your website URL to an https (HTTP over SSL), which adds additional browser protection. If you don't yet have an SSL Certificate, website visitors may not feel confident in the security of your website. Check with your website hosting company to get started.

Now that the page itself is optimized, let's move on to the donation form.

CHAPTER 12

Pre-Donation –
The Online Giving Form

Even a beautiful, donor-centric, mobile-responsive, and user-optimized online giving page can fail to convert visitors into donors if the donation form itself is not optimized.

Crafting a high converting online giving form is an art as well as a science. The form should not be thrown together on a whim or left unchanged for months and years, as technology and internet usage habits evolve and change.

Let's take a look at all of the elements of an online giving form, and how to best optimize for a maximum amount of conversions.

Contact Info and Payment Info

Don't go overboard on required content. If you ask for a lot of required information, your conversion rate could suffer. Getting payment info is a no-brainer. You can always get more info *after* the donation comes through.

The donor's name, mailing address, and email address will be required in order to successfully run a credit card transaction and to provide a receipt.

Giving the donor several options for payment types, including credit card, ACH (Automated Clearing House), and third-party merchant services like PayPal or Apple Pay, will reduce the chances that a donor will abandon the page because they do not see their preferred form of payment listed.

Beyond the options for payment, there are optional contact information fields, like phone number, preferred name, and other demographic information (gender identity, age, etc.). While there is no limit to the amount of information you could ask for on a form, there is a point in which asking too much may turn the donor off from donating to you entirely.

My advice here is two-fold:

- Collect only what you are truly going to use. Are you going to call donors? If not, don't ask for a phone number yet. Be honest with yourself about what your intentions are.

- Don't forget that you can ask for some information post-donation. The confirmation page (the page that donors are redirected to after they fill out the form) is a place where you can collect additional information.

In general, a longer form will get filled out less often than a shorter form, so don't let a form get too bloated, especially if you won't be using the information you collect anyway.

Suggested Donation Amounts
with Impact Description

Sometimes called a "gift array" or "giving ladder," suggested donation amounts take the guesswork out of the donor's mind and help
you dictate their giving level.

Not only should a form suggest gift amounts, but you should
justify the numbers you choose. For example, Coburn Place in
Indianapolis does so this way:

- $15.00 – provides one night of safe haven for an adult and
  two children.
- $50.00 – provides an Advocate to help a resident establish
  a personal plan for independence.
- $100.00 – provides a support group session to help adults
  learn the warning signs and cycle of abuse.
- $150.00 – provides a Housing Specialist to help a resident
  secure safe, permanent housing.
- $450.00 – provides one month of safe haven for a family.
- $960.00 – provides 12 hours of school break camp to all
  Coburn Place kids.
- $1,500.00 – sponsors an apartment for one year.

Stair-stepped amounts like $20, $50, $100, and $250 are
standard, but some creative organizations use unique giving
amounts, like $19, $37, $64, etc. to be more attention-grabbing.
The suggested donation amounts are one of many great things on
a donation form that you can test.

A recurring, monthly giving option is an absolute must.
According to Target Analytics, first-year monthly donors were
retained at as high as 78%.

Monthly donations also create a stickiness factor. Chances are that donors won't even notice the charges hitting their credit card or checking account. Call it the Netflix'ification of giving.

Ask to Pass on the Payment Processing Fees

My good friend Simon Scriver, CFRE, shared with us a little experiment he conducted on a donation form. He added a small checkbox that stated "Cover the Charity's Fees" that increases the donation amount by a few percentage points, covering all credit card, admin fees, etc. so that the charity walks away with the full original amount the donor was trying to give. He reported that about 10-20% of donors checked the box. Not bad!

Anonymity Option

With a checkbox, ask "Would you like to remain anonymous in agency publications?" This will cover you for print and digital materials (annual reports, social media, etc.).

Designation Option

Allowing donors to choose where their dollars will go to work empowers them. At the same time, nonprofits can show off their multitude of services and activities.

Honorarium Option

Occasionally, donors may want to make a gift in honor of someone. Providing this option will give you insights into why they give and inform your future relationship-building efforts with them.

Now that you've optimized yourself for more conversions and a better donor experience, it's time to turn your attention to the post-donation experience. How your website and online giving software communicate to that donor after a gift may be the first interaction the donor ever has with your nonprofit. It's absolutely critical that you make a positive first impression.

Unfortunately, this is one area of fundraising where stewardship is left totally up to the robots.

What online donors see immediately after filling out your donation form and clicking "donate" is totally automated by your website and online giving software. And rarely is it customized beyond the default settings.

To be clear, I'd like you to put this book down for a moment, go to your nonprofit's website, click "donate," and give $1 to yourself.

After doing so, two things are going to happen:

1. You will be redirected from your giving form to another page of your website, a "confirmation" or "thank you" page.
2. Your online giving provider will (hopefully) send some kind of email confirmation.

There is absolutely no reason why the confirmation webpage and the automated email cannot be customized to fulfill all the tenets of the donor loyalty research that we outlined earlier.

Let's dive into the confirmation page and the automatic email receipt, looking at specific content that is ideal for both.

CHAPTER 13

Post-Donation –
The "Thank You" Page

The confirmation page is the page where the donor is redirected after completing the online giving form on your donation page. The mechanics of the confirmation page can vary based on how online giving is set up on your website. For example, your donation form may simply disappear and be replaced by a confirmation message, or the user may be redirected to an entirely new webpage.

Either way, your confirmation page should do three things:
- communicate that the donation was processed successfully
- thank the donor and preview impact
- keep them on your website (so that they hopefully do something else)

The first communication after a donation is all about trust. When donors make online transactions (whether a purchase or a donation), they want to know that they just gave their credit card to a real, trustworthy entity. If after donating, the page or form simply disappears or redirects to another page, donors might think that their donations failed or worse, that their payment information was taken advantage of. You do not want donors to be constantly refreshing their inbox hoping for a confirmation email to arrive.

Make sure the confirmation page immediately communicates that the donation was successful. It goes without saying that you should also say "thank you" here.

Lastly, do what you can to ensure that the donor doesn't leave or close out of your website after viewing the confirmation page. Don't just say "thanks" and leave them hanging! Additional conversions are always good.

Before we get into the details of optimizing your confirmation page, let's first talk about its architecture.

Ideally, your confirmation page is as native to your website as your online donation page. What makes a confirmation page "native" is the fact that it has its own unique URL, like nonprofit.org/donate/thanks, just as your donation page is nonprofit.org/donate.

Not having a dedicated page can prevent you from gaining insights into the behavior of your donors and can limit your ability to cultivate them following their donations.

If you're monitoring your website traffic, you likely know the number of visits to your donation page, how visitors get there, and how long they stay. When your donation confirmation page has its own unique URL, you have the ability to gain similar insights. For example, you can identify the number of potential donors who abandon your donation page without donating. (This can be extrapolated without a dedicated confirmation page, but it's a little more difficult.)

You can also see where donors go after they reach your confirmation page. Without the dedicated page, you can't separate those who donate and continue to click through your site from those who don't donate but do continue to click throughout your site.

Most form builders allow you to customize the confirmation message following a donation, but the options are typically limited to changing the text of the message. Doing so severely limits your ability to keep the donor on your website to take another action.

This "additional action" is critical. Without it, visitors simply close your website and forget about you until the next appeal or newsletter hits their inbox. Without it, a lot of pressure will be placed on your acknowledgment email or letter to generate a new interaction.

An "additional action" may look something like giving the donor a video to watch, a blog post to read, or a survey to fill out. The goal here is to keep the donor on your website in order to generate a second, non-monetary interaction, such as registering for a volunteer outing or signing an online petition.

Being able to customize the page and track its effectiveness allows you to test and tweak page elements until you find what works best for your organization. For example, you may find that your donors are less inclined to fill out a donor survey than they are to follow you on social media, meaning you'll need to find an alternative way to generate survey responses.

If you have the ability to create and to customize your own webpages, be sure to take advantage of the redirect option.

Optimizing the Confirmation Page

Here are a few ideas for your donation confirmation page.

In this first grouping of ideas, you'll find ways to make donors feel appreciated and set them up to receive future communications from your organization. All seven of the ideas below can and should be featured on one page.

Make the Donor Feel Special

- Say "Your donation was processed successfully!" with text.
- Say "Thank you!" with text.
- Say how the donation dollars will be used with text.
- Say how the donation will impact those your organization serves (slightly different from #3) with text.
- Show the impact of their donation with a photo or photos.
- Say thanks and show the impact of their donation with a video.
- Explain in text what the donor can expect to receive from future communications.

Generate a Second Interaction

After you make donors feel all warm and fuzzy inside, you'll want to re-engage them and generate a second interaction.

The worst thing that can happen is for donors to close your website immediately after donating. You spent a lot of time and energy a) getting them to your website and b) getting them to donate. Since they're already on your website, give them something enticing to do next.

As opposed to the seven items above, you do not want to place all of the items below on one page. This would risk what Unbounce calls *The Toothpaste Trance,* meaning a website visitor is given so many options that they end up buying something at random that will end up being meaningless to them (like when you're paralyzed by all the options in the toothpaste aisle and end up choosing a random tube).

Select just a few of the ideas below that make the most sense for your organization. Whatever you choose represents excellent candidates for A/B testing.

- contact info ("Contact us any time with questions or concerns!")
- social media buttons to share that they gave
- "Follow Us/Like Us" on social media buttons
- link directly to brand social media accounts
- link to a donor survey
- link to another webpage or blog post
- link to upcoming events
- link to volunteer opportunities
- employee matching options (can be text that asks donors to check with their employer about matching gifts or a search box that searches participating companies)
- embedded contact form for feedback ("Have a question or comment? Fill out this form to let us know!")
- link or form to subscribe to blog
- create and send tribute card

Social Proof

Your donation confirmation page is also a good opportunity to reassure the donor that they are not alone and that their gift matters. You can include a:

- donor testimonial ("Why I give" and/or "Why I continue to give")
- campaign or project status

There's no reason why the confirmation page has to remain a throw-away item. Use it to put a smile on the donor's face!

While the donor is looking at your beautiful confirmation page, their inbox is likely receiving an email whose creation and deployment was totally automated. This too can be optimized!

CHAPTER 14

Post-Donation –
The Automated Email

The automatic email confirmation is an email that is automatically sent to the donor after completing the form on your donation page. This email may be generated by your website CMS, your donor database (if online giving is integrated), or your stand-alone online giving provider.

Regardless, your email receipt should do three things:
- arrive immediately
- thank the donor and preview impact
- give them something to do next

An immediate arrival of the receipt will add to the trust factor of your confirmation page: Donors will know that the transaction completed successfully.

The content of the receipt is often overlooked. Go the extra mile and craft the confirmation in a way that truly delights the donor and makes them feel involved in the mission. The thank-you should be personal and heartfelt, and it should communicate the impact of the gift and the difference that the donor makes. You can also encourage another interaction.

There's no reason why the email receipt can't keep the donor engaged and begin the process of stewarding the next gift. Improving the quality of your email confirmation is not only incredibly simple, but also easily accomplished in a matter of minutes.

Let's look at all of the individual elements of an automated donation email acknowledgment. Follow these suggestions and transform your boring receipt into a true thank you that drives additional actions!

Subject Line

Subject lines are typically perfunctory, but they don't have to be. In fact, you can have some fun and set a donor-centric tone before the recipient even opens up your email.

- Okay: "Donation receipt"
- Better: "Thank you for your donation"
- Best: "Your gift just changed a life"

The risk with the last example is that it might not clearly signify a receipt. Subject lines are a great thing to test, to measure, and to adjust.

In my $5 experiment, 46 out of the 50 organizations immediately sent me an acknowledgment via email.

Let's break down those 46 examples into a few subject line categories (with duplicates and similar examples merged for the sake of brevity):

The Bare Minimums

- Donation Receipt
- Confirmation–Donation Received
- Donation to (ORGANIZATION)
- Donation Acknowledgment
- Donation Receipt from (ORGANIZATION)

The problem: I've seen pharmacy receipts that are more enticing.

The Kinda Confusing

- Welcome to the (ORGANIZATION) online community
- (ORGANIZATION) Customer Receipt/Purchase Confirmation

The problem: The first subject line doesn't really look like a transaction receipt, and the second looks like it's having an identity crisis.

The Basic Thank-Yous

- Thank you for your donation!
- Thank you for supporting (ORGANIZATION)
- Thank You!
- Thank you for your Donation to (ORGANIZATION)!
- Thank you for your generosity!
- (ORGANIZATION) Would Like to Thank You!
- Thank you for your gift

The problem: Getting better, but still not communicating impact.

The Impacts

- Thank you! Your donation of $5.00 will advance pediatric medicine and research

The problem: Now we're talking, but could the subject line be more specific?

In general, most subject lines are very generic. Being generic is problematic for two reasons:

1. Someone just gave you money to support your mission. Why is your thank-you so boring and unexciting?

2. Spammers try to make their emails look legit, and they're getting better at it. "Thank you for your purchase" and "Thank you for your donation" are used often by spammers to make you open their fake emails. Being unique and specific will make your emails stand out from spammers.

Here are a few ideas for making your subject lines really pop:

- **Don't be afraid to write a long subject line.** According to a study by Adestra released in 2012, subject lines of 150 characters in length outperformed those in the 50-60 character range.

- **Ditch your organization name.** Because it probably already appears in the "From" field, why waste any of your precious characters?

- **Communicate impact.** What did the donation do, specifically? Try *"Your gift just fed a family of four for one week!"*

- **Get excited.** This isn't a thank-you note to your aunt for a pair of socks. Someone is helping to fund your mission!

Do These Subject Lines Matter?

When it comes to marketing emails, like newsletters and appeals, a good subject line can make or break the campaign. Email subject lines are a book cover, and people definitely judge a book by its cover.

But with receipt emails, whether from a donation or purchase, you can probably get away with being a bit perfunctory. People expect email receipts following an online transaction and will most likely open the email and save it for their records regardless of what the subject line says (so long as it clearly identifies itself).

However, an email subject line is a sneaky-good place to personalize and communicate impact to a donor—before they even read the body of the message—and do so in a fun and engaging way.

So, don't sleep on your subject lines. They are the first and perhaps the best chance to delight your donors.

From or Reply-to Address

In order to make your email look more personal, set the sender as a real email address, like john@nonprofit.org. This looks far more appealing than no-reply18590101@nonprofit.org.

Branding

Emails that look like they came from your organization, rather than a generic payment processor, are more authoritative and trustworthy. At the bare minimum, include your logo.

Personalized Greeting

The first words of your email should be a personal greeting that includes the donor's name. No personalization is better than "Dear donor," or "Thanks %%USER NAME%%!" (when bad data causes something to break).

Tone

Don't be afraid to take an informal, conversational tone in your email, unless it absolutely contradicts your brand image or voice. A thank-you email does not have to sound as bland as the note you wrote to your aunt, thanking her for that brand-new pair of socks.

Short Paragraphs

Short, scannable paragraphs improve readability and help move the recipient down through the email. If they open your email and see one giant wall of text, you can pretty much guarantee that it won't be read. Shoot for two sentences per paragraph break, three at the absolute most.

First Thank-You

The first full paragraph of your email acknowledgment should be a thank-you, and not just any thank-you. You need to shower them with the love and adoration they deserve.

Impact Statement

The second full paragraph should communicate the impact that the donation made: "Because of you, a family of four will stay warm for one week." Or, "Your $20 just supplied the vaccinations one dog needs to be eligible for adoption." Specifically stating how the dollars will be used is best, and you'll really score points if you can weave into the acknowledgment the story of one specific service recipient.

First Action Request

The third full paragraph should ask the donor to take action. This can be a new donor survey or a request for feedback on their experience as a supporter. You could even highlight volunteer opportunities or inquire about employee matching.

Second Thank-You

The fourth full paragraph should reiterate how much you appreciate the donor. Seriously, pour it on here.

Humanization

Look for opportunities to humanize your brand, perhaps through a photo of your team or a thank-you video.

Next Steps

In the case of a first-time donation, the fifth full paragraph should set expectations for what the donor should expect from you next. Remember from the research we covered previously: Donors want to know "what to expect from your organization with each interaction."

Set the stage here. Start by saying, "Over the next few weeks, you can expect to receive . . . "

If this is a returning donor, set the stage for the next immediate touch.

Close with Personal Authorship or Signature

You don't want your thank-you emails coming from your logo or brand name. Make them come from a real person, like your executive director (ghost-written is okay).

Second Action Request

Same as above, just do something different from the first action request. If the body of the email is getting a little long, you could place your words in the footer.

Tax Receipt and Organization Name

The term "tax receipt" and your organization name should appear in plain text somewhere on your email.

The donor may have to search their email inbox around tax time, long after the actual donation, to locate this document. Make it easy for them. If it's embedded in an image, the email client search tool may not pick it up.

If this email is in addition to a tax receipt email sent by the payment processor, you can skip this step–just make sure that first email is search-friendly.

Social Sharing

Consider a "Tweet your support" link that opens a pre-written tweet for the donor to send, such as *"I just donated to @Nonprofit-Name and you should too >>> (link)."*

"Click to Tweet" is a simple and free tool for creating pre-written tweet links.

Recommending that the donor follow you on social media is also a prudent ask.

Subscription Options

Because this email is a transaction-based email, the email is exempt from CAN-SPAM regulations and you are not required to offer an unsubscribe option. However, it is a best practice to offer a "manage email preferences" option that includes unsubscribe.

Speed

If the automated email is the only acknowledgment and includes the tax receipt, the email should come within minutes of completing the donation. If the automated email is a follow-up to a separate tax receipt, it can come hours later (but the same day is best).

Size

Strive to keep the file size of your email as small as possible, as this is a trigger for spam filters. *Email on Acid* recently found that the optimum size is somewhere between 15 kbs and 100 kbs.

Avoiding too many images is the best way to keep your file size down.

Don't sleep on your automatic email confirmations. They don't have to look like something you get from the pharmacy!

Here are your quick tips:

1. Remove the word "receipt" from the subject line. You did not just sell a gallon of milk. You received a donation.

2. Change the sender from a role-based email (like finance@ nonprofit.org) to an email address belonging to an actual human. Donors give to humans, not robots. Check the sender name as well, and make sure it is either your organization's name or a staff member's name.

3. If your email does not include tax information, add a note that says you'll be sending that shortly. Don't give your donors any reason to worry.

4. Put a donor-centric outpouring of appreciation, which also includes an explanation of how the donation will be used, as close to the top of the email as you can.

5. Say thank you. Multiple times. You'd be surprised how few of these emails actually do.

6. Let the donor know what comes next (an email newsletter, a letter in the mail, etc.).

7. Give donors something to do next, like visit your Facebook page or watch a video. You already have their attention, so capitalize on it!

Even though you now have optimized online giving pages, donation forms, confirmation pages, and automated email receipts, your work isn't done yet. In fact, your work should never be done.

It's time to test, and test some more!

CHAPTER 15

Continuous Improvement through A/B Testing

External advice and your own assumptions will only get you so far.

The best way to know if your online giving pages are converting visitors at the highest possible rate is to frequently test and tweak those pages.

If your website or online giving provider allows for A/B testing, take advantage of it! If they don't, you can use a free tool called Google Optimize to experiment with multiple variations of the same page while measuring the results of each iteration.

There are several elements you can test.

On the Webpage

- headlines
- paragraph text
- images
- calls to action

The text and images on your page can have a huge effect on whether or not your sign-up and donation forms get filled out. Be sure to test headlines, paragraph text, and any images. Consider placement and arrangement as well. Make sure nothing distracts from or pushes the form below the fold. You don't want people to have to scroll to get to the form.

CTAs, or calls to action, are also very important to consider and test. These, like buttons, should be compelling and encourage an action. User experience is paramount here. For example, "click here" as a text link isn't a great CTA, since some of your visitors may be using a mobile device. Plus, it's not very compelling. As with your buttons, try something like "give now" or "support us now."

Your forms can also be tested.

In the Form

- form length (quantity of questions asked)
- suggested gift amounts / giving ladder
- field size
- field questions
- premiums

Keep in mind that the shorter the form, the more completions it typically gets. Don't ask too many questions, or you might scare off the website visitor. The drawback is you get less information about the donor to work with.

You can also test the verbiage of the questions. What happens if you ask for "Phone Number" instead of "Cell Phone Number?"

If you offer premiums, you can test different options. If you don't offer premiums, what would happen if you did?

The suggested gift amounts (if you have them) represent one of the best elements for testing in any fundraising efforts, not just online giving.

For example, you could test two form variations where the lowest suggested dollar amount is $20 on one and $10 on the other. You may find that when $20 is the lowest option, it gets just as many donations as the $10 variation, meaning you would net more if the lowest option was always $20. In general, donors will gravitate to the lowest suggested amount, and testing can help you find the "sweet spot" that generates the most revenue before turning the donor off completely.

In the Follow-Up

Everything on the confirmation/thank-you page can also be tested and honed.

For example, one variation of the page could direct donors to an events calendar, while one directs donors to volunteer opportunities. Or, both variations could include a survey question that is worded differently for each. Which gets the most answers?

The possibilities are limitless, and you'll never know which option or combination of options results in the highest engagement until you test for yourself.

Before we conclude the online giving section of this book, let's look at one of the fastest growing sub-segments of online giving: peer-to-peer (P2P).

CHAPTER 16

Peer-To-Peer

One could argue that peer-to-peer (P2P) fundraising should just be called fundraising.

After all, people give to people, so isn't all good fundraising peer-to-peer fundraising?

For the sake of not muddying the waters, modern day peer-to-peer fundraising deserves attention. It sits at the intersection of all the channels we've discussed—analog and digital, social media, and online giving—and is now widely used within the sector.

Although analog peer-to-peer fundraising has been around for decades, our digital age allows fans of any cause to create personal fundraising pages that can be promoted globally within minutes—all at little cost to the nonprofit that benefits from the donations.

Low acquisition rates only tell half the story. The other side of this double-edged sword is lower donor retention rates. For P2P donors, it's not uncommon for rates to be in the single digit percentages.

Why is this happening, and what can we do about it?

The answer lies in the name itself: peer-to-peer. The retention rates between the peer and the organization are low because the organization isn't part of the equation.

Allow me to illustrate.

Let's say it's my birthday, and I create a birthday fundraiser on Facebook and ask all of my Facebook friends to donate. The organization I am choosing to support is the local breast milk bank where my wife works. Our extended family experienced a few premature births and we understand the value of an organization like that.

Luckily, I have a very generous network, and I quickly raised $1,000 from a few dozen friends.

Let's also pretend for a moment that the breast milk bank gets the name and contact info of all the donors (it won't if the campaign was a Facebook fundraiser). What do they do if they're like most organizations? They send a rote thank-you and bombard them with marketing messages going forward. Meanwhile I, the fundraiser, am not thanked or soft credited for raising those funds.

In the case of not receiving the contact info of the donors, what does the organization do? It agonizes over that fact, unaware that those people will probably never give again, even if you acquired their contact info.

In a peer-to-peer fundraising campaign, it's important that the human fundraiser is being supported, *not* the benefiting organization. The donor may not even know what the benefiting organization is or care about what they do.

And what happens when the organization swoops in and acts like those donors are their biggest fans?

Confusion, annoyance, and alienation.

All the while, the person you should be showering with attention—the fundraiser—goes under-acknowledged. So, what can you do to make your peer-to-peer efforts truly shine?

Focus on the Positives

Yes, many peer-to-peer donors are going to be "one and done." But your cost to acquire their gifts was pretty low, and you've identified a rabid supporter (the fundraiser).

Focus on the Fundraiser

Make sure that donors are acknowledged for what they did. After all, they did most of the heavy fundraising lifting for you. A handwritten note, a video message, or a phone call is definitely in order. Don't forget to soft credit all the gifts to them in your donor database!

Contextualize Your Follow-Up with the Donor

Don't be afraid to re-introduce your organization to the donor in your gift acknowledgment and be sure to reference the fundraiser so that they know why they're getting this acknowledgment. Because of how easy it is to donate to a P2P campaign, you really cannot underestimate the likelihood that donors will have no memory of doing so!

Check out one of the best P2P acknowledgments I ever received. It checks all the boxes, and adroitly asks for additional engagement.

Subject: Hello from Coburn Place!

Hi Steven!

I'm Julie Henson, the Community Engagement Director at Coburn Place and I got connected to you through Adam

Clevenger and your generous participation in his birthday fundraiser!! Woo! You all really hit it out of the park and have impacted Coburn Place in a big way. We also use Bloomerang here at Coburn Place and love it, so definitely grateful to you for that!

I wanted to write for two reasons. One, I'd love to get you in for a tour and show you around so you can see firsthand the impact you're having through participating in Adam's fundraiser, and through having awesome software that helps us keep track of all the good stuff. And secondly, Adam mentioned that Bloomerang often does volunteer days. We love having corporate groups out to do all sorts of projects, and I'd love to chat and see if that would be something your crew would be interested in doing. We have dates open throughout the year and plenty of versatile projects!

Thanks so much for your time and generosity! I look forward to chatting!

Julie Henson

Community Engagement Director

Coburn Place

Peer-to-peer is at high risk of becoming robotic, transactional, and impersonal. The worst thing you can do is lump all of your P2P donors into the same communications that your "direct" donors get.

They are inherently a different kind of donor and need to be treated as such. And as P2P fundraising becomes more prevalent, savvy organizations will have specialized P2P communications at the ready, like Coburn Place does.

Now that you have some good practice in human-centered optimization of your online fundraising channels, let's look at how to optimize your outbound communications.

The first distraction is everyone's favorite: email!

Part IV

EMAIL MARKETING

Email joins social media and online giving as the final member of the digital trinity most susceptible to the pitfalls of an untrained handler.

Prior to the emergence and ubiquity of email marketing, nonprofits needed to engage multiple skilled practitioners in order to communicate en masse with constituents: a designer, a copywriter, a printer, and a mail house.

Now, anyone can log into any number of email marketing providers and send a message in less time than it takes to pick up a latte in the drive-through line.

As with any other technology tool, mass email marketing comes with the power to generate thousands of dollars in revenue. But in the hands of the untrained, mass email marketing also comes with the power to ruin a long-term relationship—or squelch one before it even has the chance to grow—with just a couple of clicks of the mouse.

Why? It's a dangerous combination of lack of respect for the tool and an overreliance on a one-size-fits-all approach.

Consider the following:

- Email is not a replacement for direct mail, no matter how young or old your current or future recipients are.

- The email newsletter is not the next stage in evolution of the print newsletter.
- Email marketing should be taken as seriously as grant writing.
- Lack of segmentation rears its ugly head digitally most often in the form of email.
- The robots aren't yet sophisticated enough to leave all the decisions to them.

In this section, we'll cover several elements of email marketing that are too often left to the robots. The human touch is still possible over email—it just takes some work, a bit of creativity, and a whole lot of reverence for the power of the tool.

Speaking of reverence, let's quickly examine the rules of sending mass emails so that you stay out of trouble. Robots don't care about getting in trouble.

CHAPTER 17

When You Can and
Can't Send a Mass Email

Many organizations (nonprofit and for-profit) get themselves into trouble, legally and by reputation, for abusing email. Whether it's a solicitation or an innocuous organization update, many emails and newsletters can find themselves in a spam folder faster than you can hit send.

These issues typically stem from a misunderstanding of who and how you can and cannot email, even after procuring an email address.

Understanding Opt-Ins

When someone freely gives you their email address, they can fall into one of two categories of "permission:"

- Express permission. They give you their email address because they want and expect to receive emails from you.

- Implied permission. A transaction occurs that involves an exchange of email addresses (such as a donation or a business card exchange).

With *express permission*, users may visit your website and sign up for your newsletter. An email confirmation takes place, and they are added to your list. This is sometimes referred to as a confirmed opt-in.

Implied permission scenarios are typically unconfirmed opt-ins. For example, someone may give you a business card, and you email them later. There was no explicit request to be emailed, but they did give you their address.

In either case, you should follow CAN-SPAM guidelines. It should be noted that the CAN-SPAM Act exempts "transactional or relationship messages." In other words, if someone donates and gives you their email address, you are free to email them, even without expressly stating that you will email them. However, you should also employ email best practices to ensure that the recipient does not become fatigued or irritated by your emails, resulting in an unsubscribe or spam report.

For nonprofits, there are many different scenarios through which you could receive an email address. Here are a few of the most common ones and the actions you should and should not take for each.

Someone signed up via our website to receive our email newsletter. Can we email them? Yes.

This is about the safest opt-in you will receive. However, if you want to make sure that the subscriber does not unsubscribe and stays engaged, be sure to give them the opportunity to sign up for one or more topic-specific newsletters, not one generic newsletter.

Having multiple subscription lists will ensure that you deliver only the content they are interested in receiving.

Someone donated via our website. We asked for their email address and they gave it to us. Can we email them? Yes, but . . .

You should do two things:

- On the sign-up form, explicitly state that by giving you their email address, they are agreeing to receive emails from you.
- Only send them donor-centric emails–up until they signal interest in other types of content.

Someone signed up via our website to become a volunteer. We asked for their email address and they gave it to us. Can we email them? Yes, but . . .

You should do two things:

- On the sign-up form, explicitly state that by giving you their email address, they are agreeing to receive emails from you.
- Only send them volunteer-centric emails–up until they signal interest in other types of content.

A non-donor/non-volunteer gave us their email address via a physical sign-up form at an event. Can we email them? Yes, but . . .

As advised above, you should clearly state on the form that by giving you their email address, they are agreeing to receive emails from you. Be sure to only send them relevant emails.

A board member gave our development staff a business card of someone they thought might be interested in the organization. Can we email them? Sort of.

You cannot (should not) add them to your bulk newsletter list. However, you could email them individually. Explain how you received the business card and attempt to create and nurture the relationship. Only after they officially opt-in or donate can you add them to a bulk list.

A donor responded to a direct mail appeal and included their email address. We did not have an email address for them prior. Can we email them? Yes, but . . .

Once again, you should clearly state on the form that by giving you their email address, they are agreeing to receive emails from you. Only send them donor-centric emails. If they donated, they would fall within the transactional relationship-type, and CAN-SPAM regulations would not apply. However, they could still choose to mark your emails as spam if they are not relevant or engaging.

We collected business cards in a fishbowl at an event as part of a raffle. Can we email them? Yes, but . . .

You can expect a high unsubscribe rate and spam reports if you immediately add them to your bulk list and start sending generic newsletters. It would be better to email them individually first and gauge their true interest.

A similar or partner nonprofit offered to share their list with us. Can we email them? No.

Those subscribers opted-in to receive emails from the sharing organization, not yours. Because no opt-in occurred, the CAN-SPAM Act prohibits this.

We bought a list of email addresses. Can we email them? No.

Because no opt-in occurred, the CAN-SPAM Act prohibits this.

Our major gift officer pulled some email addresses of people whom they might want to contact off of a corporate website. Can we email them? No, but . . .

You *could* email them individually. However, don't expect a high success rate. Because no opt-in occurred, the CAN-SPAM Act prohibits adding these addresses to your bulk list.

We purchased an email append service. Can we email the updated addresses? Probably.

As long as you can verify that the email addresses belong to the subscriber for whom you previously had an email address for, via a legitimate opt-in, *and* that person has not unsubscribed.

Follow these scenario guidelines to keep yourself out of trouble, and more importantly, out of the spam folder.

CHAPTER 18

Email Deliverability and Spam Filters

Spam filters are the bane of many email marketers across all industry types. Even the most well-intentioned, authentic, and law-abiding emails can still find their way into a recipient's spam folder, with or without their knowledge or intent.

At the same time, some emails are so irrelevant, ill-timed, and poorly crafted that the recipient can't help but mark it as spam.

Because it is such an affordable and powerful communications option for nonprofits, fundraisers should pay close attention to best practices and legal guidelines when sending any bulk email.

Yes, it's literally the law!

In 2003, the CAN-SPAM Act was signed into law. The bill requires compliance on the part of all organizations who send commercial (marketing) emails. Relational or transactional emails to existing customers (donors) or anyone who has inquired about the organization's services are exempted. However, those emails are also routinely marked as spam.

As such, there are still things you can do to prevent your subscribers from marking your messages as spam, whether it's a solicitation, newsletter/update, or an acknowledgment.

- Only email someone who has opted-in to receive emails from you.
- Do not purchase lists.
- Do not pull email addresses off websites and add them to your list.
- If a friend, employee, or board member gives you the email address of a prospective donor, do not add that email address to your bulk list until you have permission (make contact separately and individually first).
- Include an unsubscribe option, and always honor unsubscribe requests.
- Include your physical address and a phone number.
- Always explain why the recipient is receiving the message (explain how you acquired the email address).

The CAN-SPAM Act also requires that you do not use misleading or deceptive subject lines. In other words, the content of your subject line must be relative to the body content of the email. For example, you can't use a subject line like "Hurricane Evacuation Notice" when the email is just your general monthly newsletter.

Technical Requirements

Here are a few best practices and technical requirements to keep in mind when sending emails.

Send from a domain email address, not an internet service provider or third-party email vendor. Make sure you use an email address associated with your domain, like @yourdomain.org, and not something like @gmail.com, @aol.com or @comcast.net email address.

Don't send from a role-based email address. Sending from addresses like noreply@yourdomain.org, info@yourdomain.org or newsletter@yourdomain.org should be avoided. Instead, try to send from a real person with a real email address, like paul@yourdomain.org.

Keep the size of the email small. Some email programs and spam filters consider the size of the email as a spam trigger. If you use images in an email, make sure they are properly sized for the web, and avoid sending attachments.

Ask your recipients to white label you. Many of your email recipients may not even know that your emails are being marked as spam. Filters found in email programs such as Outlook or IT infrastructure and firewalls at a corporate office may block your messages. Ask your subscribers to add your sending address to their address book or preferred recipients list.

For those US-based nonprofits fundraising in the European Union, GDPR (General Data Protection Regulation) compliance is a must. While it's likely that your technology vendors have made the necessary changes to stay in compliance with the EU's data privacy regulations, it's never a bad idea to bring it up to them or consult with your legal representative.

Content Best Practices

Though there are many technical missteps to avoid, the biggest factor in whether or not a recipient marks your email as spam is the content of the email.

Send good emails. This may seem like either unhelpful advice or a no-brainer, but many nonprofits are still sending irrelevant messages to their email list. One way to avoid this is to set up multiple subscription lists. For example, rather than having one newsletter that you send to everyone, consider creating a donor newsletter, a volunteer newsletter and/or a services newsletter. If someone signs up to be a volunteer, it doesn't make much sense to send them information on planned giving.

By segmenting your audience, you have a better chance of sending relevant messages, which will cut down on instances of emails being reported as spam.

Avoid all-caps, symbols and punctuation marks in subject lines. A bad subject line is ">>> DONATE NOW!!! <<<" A good subject line is "You can make a difference today."

Avoid trigger words in subject lines. Many studies have been conducted on what words trigger spam filters. A quick Google search for "subject line words that trigger spam" will get you a variety of studies that typically center around the kinds of words you might see on late-night television infomercials.

It's important to take all studies with a grain of salt and to continually test your emails for performance.

Offer both an HTML and plain text version of your emails. Some recipients set their email clients to only accept plain text emails. If your HTML email doesn't have a plain text version, it won't be received.

Don't include too many links. If your emails are segmented, targeted and short, this shouldn't be an issue. If you're sending to your entire list a bulk, generic newsletter that touches on many different topics and includes a dozen or more links, you're probably going to get marked as spam.

A 100% avoidance of spam filters is probably going to be impossible for your nonprofit organization. Many for-profits have entire teams of email marketing experts who spend hours testing and tweaking messages, and they still don't avoid the spam filter every time. With the multitude and diversity of ISPs (Internet Service Providers), security systems and email clients, avoiding the spam filter is just not possible.

Be sure to adhere to all of the CAN-SPAM guidelines and to as many of the best practices in this chapter as you can. Don't get too discouraged by individual email performance—email works best as part of a multi-channel strategy that includes direct mail, personal contact, and other online channels like social media.

Now that you know how best to send, let's talk about when and what to send.

CHAPTER 19

Email Scheduling

The ability to schedule emails through an email marketing tool can be a powerful addition to any communications toolkit. But as with most technology, there's a danger that it can also encourage and reinforce bad habits.

From a nonprofit marketing perspective, here are three common use cases for scheduling emails that can be problematic.

You've always sent this kind of email at that date and time. So, you've just acquired the ability to schedule emails, and you're excited about the increased productivity that comes with being able to schedule your email newsletter for a set date on your calendar.

Before you get too caught up in your new-found power, take a step back and ask yourself, "Why do we send this newsletter at this same date and time every month?"

Has this ever been questioned? Or, like so many other nonprofit practices, do you just do it because that's the way it's always been done?

Unless you have some data to back up the assertion that this is absolutely the best date and time to send this particular email, and that's why you do it, then it should be re-evaluated and tested.

Having the ability to schedule emails is a great introduction into the world of A/B testing, whether it's manual or automated, as well as data segmentation. Consider segmenting your list into several groups and testing different send times. But don't get too wrapped up in the results. Remember: date and time of sending is not the only factor that impacts open rates. Subject lines and the sender's name can have an even greater impact, so be sure to test those as well.

An arbitrary but strict schedule can also lead to bad content. For example, let's say your monthly newsletter goes out on the 15th of the month at 10:00 a.m. no matter what. The 14th of the month rolls around and—even though the email is scheduled—you haven't populated it with content. So, you scramble to manufacture or cobble together content that ends up falling flat. A bad email is worse than an unsent email.

Besides, no one is staring at their inbox at 8:57 a.m. waiting in anticipation for your 9:00 a.m. newsletter. A slight schedule change will probably go completely unnoticed by recipients.

You read an article or a study that says the best time to send is 9:00 a.m. on a Wednesday (or whenever). Data is great, and benchmark studies can be extremely valuable in guiding your strategic efforts. But both should not be the deciding factors for determining the best strategy.

Many benchmark studies directly contradict one another, which can lead to confirmation bias. In other words, it's easy to find a study that backs up your preconceived notions on the best strategies.

The reason these studies differ from one another so frequently is that the audiences being studied vary greatly. Your audience is going to be different than the audiences being reported on in the study. What worked for them won't necessarily work for your audience, which is why constantly testing different strategies on your unique audience is so important.

But let's say, just for fun, that there's one benchmark study that trumps all others and offers the absolute best recommendation on when to send an email. If everyone starts to follow that advice, will it not become the worst date and time to send an email? It's a noisy world, and marketers of all types are clamoring for attention from consumers. Strive to stand out from the crowd, rather than getting lost in it.

You're going on vacation and you want something to be sent out while you're gone. There may be times when you are physically unable to send an email at the desired date and time. A time-sensitive message that you schedule in advance because you won't be around to send it is a very good reason to schedule an email!

But there's another factor that we have yet to dive into: the concept of delaying content.

Let's say you've crafted a monthly newsletter with great stories of service impact and donor recognition. It's well-designed, well-written and has all the technical elements it needs to be successful. It's now scheduled to go out in two weeks, and you can cross it off your to-do list.

But . . . is there any reason to wait two weeks to send it?

If you've got great stories to tell, why wait? Now, if it's Saturday at 3:00 a.m. when you become aware of this story, then perhaps you should wait (Or should you? Check the data!). But if not, is there really a good reason not to get that out right away?

Just as a strict schedule can lead to bad content, it can also hold good content hostage!

With great power comes great responsibility, so before you blindly use a new tool just because you can, first ask yourself how you can best use that tool.

CHAPTER 20

Personalization and Merge Tags in Mass Emails

If you're like anyone with an office job, you're probably going to write dozens of emails in a day, each to an individual recipient. Mix in a few personal emails, and you'll quickly find that a large chunk of your day is spent crafting the subject lines for those emails. Subject lines are intended to get the recipient's attention so that they open your email.

I am guessing that out of all of the individual emails you'll send today, none of them will include the recipient's first name in the subject line. Unless you are mad at the person you are emailing, this just isn't a normal stylistic choice when it comes to one-to-one digital communication.

However, when it comes to mass marketing emails, there is a strange desire to do this through the use of merge tags.

What Are Merge Tags?

This is the practice of inserting a small line of code into written communication that pulls from a separate data set.

For example, you could insert a tag like |FNAME| into a letter, and when the letter is printed, the |FNAME| will be replaced by the recipient's first name. It's a great way to mass-edit documents.

Fundraisers have been using mail merges for decades, but modern marketers have more recently adopted the practice in digital communications.

One staple of this is adding merge tags to emails, specifically in email subject lines.

There's probably a few of these emails sitting in your inbox right now, like:

"Steven, our sale ends in 12 hours!"

"Steven, singles in your area want to meet you!" (They don't.)

"Steven, your donation is needed!"

With all the tools available to the modern fundraiser, an old adage still rings true: Just because we can do something doesn't mean we should. Using merge tags in fundraising email subject lines is one of my favorite shiny objects to avoid.

Here are a few reasons why. There is mixed evidence to suggest this practice produces results. A 2015 study by MarketingSherpa found that including a name in the subject line, along with other personalization, boosted open rates in *some* industries.

However, a 2008 study by Mailchimp found the exact opposite. Additionally, Benchmark Email "does not advocate adding a contact's first name in the subject line of your emails. Doing so may lead to an increase of spam complaints, as spammers are known for using personal data in the subject line of emails."

There is a more contemporary, albeit anecdotal, case study to consider: The immensely successful 2012 email fundraising campaign by then President Obama, which helped raise $690 million. This campaign is frequently cited and dissected as a model to emulate.

The methods of the 2016 Clinton presidential campaign, however, while moderately successful, drew the ire of the online community and resulted in the creation of an embarrassing meme.

While Obama made use of short, to-the-point subject lines, Clinton favored more "personalized" subject lines and body text that included merge tags.

Here are some of Obama's subject lines:

- Dinner?
- Hey
- If you're ready
- Aloha
- Today
- So
- Are you in?

Contrast these subject lines to Clinton's subject lines, which aggressively used the recipient's first name much to the chagrin of some recipients:

- Right now, (first name)
- I'm not kidding, (first name)
- What are we going to do?
- We might not win tonight, (first name)

The comparison is less about why Obama's emails worked better overall (there are a lot of reasons) and more about why

Clinton's didn't: They're just kind of annoying. It's weird to have someone you don't actually know—who isn't even the *real* sender—address you by name over and over.

The one and only purpose of a subject line is to get the recipient to open the email and not to have them feel like they were deceived. To do this, your goal should be to create urgency by telling a micro story. Merge tags that pull in first names rarely contribute to this end.

It's true that using someone's name in speech and print material does draw them in and create urgency, but my impression of using a name in a subject line is that it comes off as inauthentic—people know it's the result of a line of code!—and negates any urgency created.

In addition to the perception that merge tags can create, there's also the risk of a technical malfunction. Bad data equals embarrassing results. There are so many ways using merge tags in an email subject line can go wrong, most of which stem from your data letting you down. But let's first assume your data is clean and perfect.

Let's say your email provider uses "|FNAME|" to pull the recipient's first name from your database into the subject line.

Imagine that, while crafting your email subject line, you accidentally delete or omit the | at the end of |FNAME|, and fire off the email before noticing.

Now, all of your recipients are going to get an email that says "|FNAME, we need your help!"

Do you think that email will result in donations?

Yes, merge tags can go wrong in multiple communication mediums, but the email subject line is singularly wrought with landmines. Unlike a printed piece, which you can check before sending, there's no way to preview that all 1,000 of your mass emails are correct.

In addition to taking up valuable space, the merge tag itself sits right next to the rest of the subject line content (as opposed to a salutation in the body text that is isolated). This makes it more likely that you accidentally encroach on the tag and delete or overwrite something that makes it work.

Lastly, let's assume that you're a typical nonprofit that has some imperfect data, in the form of:

- misspelled first name
- incorrect first name
- a formal name only and not the preferred name

Your |FNAME|, even if populated with content, can still alienate the recipient.

There's little reason to take the risk for little-to-no-upside.

Don't personalize. Individualize.

Why are we trying to make mass emails look like a personal email, crafted just for the recipient? People give to people, not to robots. When you send a "personalized" mass email, you're still essentially sending an email from your logo. A logo that knows the recipient's name. If a logo walked up to me on the street (weird) and knew my name (even weirder), I would be creeped out.

There's an easy way to personalize an email. You don't need email marketing software to do it. You can just fire up Outlook or Gmail and write an email. You don't even need any training to do it. Imagine the impact of an email written by and sent from an executive director to one donor (that addresses the donor by name, is contextual based on what we know about that donor) asking for help. This email would immediately stand out in an inbox full of mass marketing emails sent by robots trying to act like humans.

Don't get me wrong; mass emails are great and can be very effective. But "personalization" isn't going to save a bad email.

Make individualization your goal, not personalization.

CHAPTER 21

Why the Sender's Email Address Matters

When auditing email communications, there is a lot to consider: the timing of the send, the subject line, the style and branding of the email, and of course, the content of the email itself.

But there's one small detail that is often overlooked: the sender's email address.

Why It Matters

Every email has to come from somewhere, and in the case of a mass or automated email, the sender's address can be specified.

The sender's email address is one of the primary elements of an email's content, second only to the subject line. And while it may seem like a small detail, it can have a deep, albeit subconscious, impact on the recipient.

What is a Role-Based Email?

A role-based email is an email address assigned to a department or a purpose, rather than a human user. For example, info@nonprofit. org is an example of a role-based email, as opposed to something like sally@nonprofit.org.

Typically, organizations will employ a role-based email when they want to send out information on behalf of the corporate entity, but not necessarily want to receive responses or to make one single person responsible for receiving those responses.

It's typical for mass emails, announcements, updates and transactional emails to come from a role-based address, but savvy organizations are wising up.

Why are Role-Based Addresses Bad?

There are many technical reasons to avoid role-based addresses. For example, they often trigger spam filters, and many email clients and providers reject them outright. It's also hard to moderate replies to emails coming from a generic mailbox.

However, for nonprofits, there is an even more compelling reason to avoid them: they're impersonal.

If you agree with the adage that "people give to people, not charities," then avoiding role-based addresses is a must. After all, can you really consider an appeal or a gift acknowledgment as personal when it comes from info@nonprofit.org? What's more, how can a donor reply or get in touch with you? Will they really feel as though there's an open line of communication?

In most cases, you can specify the sender's name and email address as two separate elements:

- from: Steven from Bloomerang
- mailto: steven@bloomerang.com

Here are some role-based addresses that you should absolutely avoid sending emails from:

- no-reply@
- info@
- development@
- fundraising@
- (organization-name)@
- or something missional like hope@, relief@, change@, etc.

What If I Want to Protect an Employee's Email Address?

It's fair to not want to publicly display or distribute a high-ranking employee's (like an executive director's or CEO's) email address.

If you absolutely can't share their email address publicly, consider creating a new address that looks like theirs but is slightly different.

For example, if your CEO's day-to-day working email address is sally.smith@nonprofit.org, consider using sally@nonprofit.org as the sender of an appeal, newsletter or acknowledgment.

If you do this, be sure to diligently moderate the inbox for any replies or important messages.

Are Role-Based Email Addresses Ever Useful or Appropriate?

Role-based email addresses are certainly useful in cases where you want to receive emails, but not necessarily send them. For example, listing volunteer@nonprofit.org on your volunteer page is one way to get people to email you. However, you'll likely find that a real person's email address (who is responsible for that campaign, fund, event, etc.) will be warmer and inviting.

Now that you've got all of the technical details down, let's look at optimizing the most common email that nonprofits send: the e-newsletter.

CHAPTER 22

Making Your
Email Newsletter Stand Out

Email newsletters are a great way to keep your supporters and constituents informed about all the happenings, needs, and triumphs of your nonprofit.

One of the hardest things about regularly distributing an email newsletter is generating content. Regardless of its delivery system (email, social, blog, etc.), content is tough to create for folks who don't get excited about a blank Word doc or a video camera staring them in the face.

Because content creation can be so taxing on your time and energy, it's always a shame when an email newsletter is the only place that content exists.

So, let's start thinking about email newsletters differently.

For most nonprofits, an email newsletter is like a stork delivery. The stork is email as the distribution channel and the newsletter is the expertly wrapped newborn baby just waiting to be delivered. That baby only gets delivered once, and when it does, it now only exists in the hands of the recipient.

Let's imagine your email newsletter contains an original article by your executive director, a few bits of news about your organization, a story about someone you serve, and a few advertisements for upcoming events. The shelf life and exposure of the content in this email newsletter is very limited, especially if all of this content was 1) written expressly for your newsletter and 2) only exists in your newsletter. In other words, the content is trapped here. Furthermore, you can only gauge the success of the email newsletter by delivery rates and email open rates, all of which hardly communicate what content was read, skimmed over, or ignored.

Rather than a stork, what if your email newsletter was a subway train, which moves recipients from their email inbox to your website?

Ideally, the article from your executive director, recent news, stories, and other pieces of content **should be written for and reside on your website first.** When this happens, your newsletter should simply **direct recipients to** the content, rather than hold the content itself.

All of this is ideal for a number of reasons.

1. That content can be consumed by more than just your email subscribers. This includes organic website visitors, referral website visitors, social media followers, etc. Don't hold your content hostage!

2. You can track its effectiveness. When your newsletter contains teaser links to content, rather than the full content itself, you can track what gets clicked, and therefore measure how interesting it is to recipients. This way, you can begin to hone your content and discard what doesn't get clicks.

3. You can convert website visitors. Given the investment in content creation, one of the worst things that can happen is for a newsletter recipient to read an article and then trash the email. There's nothing else for them to do! However, if they are directed to your website to read the article, you can include a call to action to take the next step (maybe it's a donation, sign-up, or registration).

If you're blogging, use your newsletter to get people to visit your blog. If you're creating videos, infographics, or podcasts, embed that content on your website and send newsletter subscribers to them. If you want to update people on recent news about your charity, have a recent news page (or blog category) on your site and send people there. Differing calls to action (apply today, read more, check it out) are enticing and offer variety to the reader.

I often see nonprofits who republish their newsletter on their website after it's been sent. Let's do the opposite! Start adding content regularly to your website and use email to deliver people to it, rather than delivering content to them.

After all, that stork is probably getting tired.

One Word to Avoid in Your Email Newsletter Subject Line

It's "newsletter."

Let me preface this by saying that if you send out a recurring (weekly, monthly, etc.) email newsletter with the word "newsletter" in the subject line and you're getting amazing open rates, there's no need to run out and change everything you're doing. But if you think those open rates could be better, keep reading.

Why to Say No to "Newsletter"

What is the purpose of an email subject line? In my opinion, it serves only one purpose: to get the recipient to open the email. With that goal in mind, a subject line should be enticing and perhaps even provocative, while remaining true to the content of the email. So, when your nonprofit's email newsletter has a subject line of "(Nonprofit Name) January 20xx Newsletter" are you enticing the recipient to open the email?

With the amount of email we're inundated with on a daily basis, getting another "newsletter" feels like work; reading it becomes like a task to complete.

The other reason to avoid using "newsletter" in your subject line is that it allows you to shift the focus away from your organization and onto the recipient. Assuming your newsletter contains stories of donor impact, you can use the subject line to preview those stories. For example, a hunger relief organization—instead of sending "(Nonprofit Name) January 20xx Newsletter"—could send "Read about the family you fed this month."

In Defense of "Newsletter"

Valid opposing arguments include the following:
- It lets recipients know exactly what the email is
- It helps us organize / immediately identify email campaigns in our system

A good way to accomplish both would be to "brand" your newsletter.

For example, the nonprofit Keep Indianapolis Beautiful brands its newsletter as "Get the Dirt."

Similar to the name of a publication like a magazine, "Get the Dirt" reminds the reader that this is a recurring communication while also previewing the content – all while cleverly staying "on-brand" by tying the name of the newsletter to the organization's mission.

The Prairie Center, an addiction recovery organization, does both: branding their newsletter "The Prairie Center Connector" and using provocative subject lines like, "There's a closeness we have I never did when I was their age" and "Packaging mirth, merriment, sobriety, and support during the holidays." The Prairie Center does a good job of tying the subject line directly to stories found in the newsletter.

All in all, open rates should drive your decision. If you're struggling with low open rates, the subject line should be the first thing to look at changing. And if the word "newsletter" drives that subject line content, you now have some alternative strategies to try.

Before we close the email section of this book, I want to leave you with some parting thoughts about one last type of automated email: out-of-office emails.

CHAPTER 23

Turning Away Donors with Automated Out-of-Office Emails

Imagine you're a donor who has a question to ask, feedback to share, or even a large gift to make. You fire up your email and send a message to the fundraiser or someone you know at the organization, only to receive one of the automatic response types below:

- My email address has changed from jane@nonprofit.org to janesmith@nonprofit.org. Please resend your message and change this in your contact information so that I may receive your correspondence.

- jane@nonprofit.org is no longer employed. Please email sallyjones@nonprofit.org.

- I will be on vacation from Sept. 1st to Sept. 12th. I will reply to your message as soon as possible.

- ##- Please type your reply above this line -## We're working on your request (35076). We will be in touch soon. To add additional comments, reply to this email.

You've likely received an automatic email reply like one of the above from a for-profit, particularly before or after a transaction. These emails are the equivalent of Ned Ryerson from *Groundhog Day* mocking you until the end of time.

Luckily, the solution is simple.

Set Up Email Forwarding

No matter what service you use for email, whether it's through your website hosting, Gmail, or another service, you likely have the ability to set up email forwarding.

If you change your email address, forward the old email address to the new. Don't make your donor jump through hoops because you made a change. If an employee leaves, forward emails sent to them to another employee. That employee can respond to any issues personally.

If you are going on vacation for an extended amount of time, consider forwarding your emails to another employee (if in a similar role) or at least give them the contact info for someone who can help them immediately.

If you are using a generic, role-based email address to collect inquiries or make broad announcements, STOP! Humans give to humans, not robots. Give your email recipients the ability to reply to another human immediately.

Remember an earlier point in this book when DonorVoice found that the fourth highest reason why donors stay loyal is that they "receive opportunities to make their views known?"

If you are not giving supporters this ability, their loyalty may diminish or never even get established.

There are far too many robots involved in fundraising, from role-based email addresses to automated receipts, that make donors feel like an ATM rather than a partner in your cause.

It is normal to feel overwhelmed by all this email advice but remember: No one knows your audience better than you do. First and foremost, lean on past experience for guidance. Look back on past emails and investigate which subject lines performed best for your intended purpose. If you can't find a clear winner, consider experimenting with some of the ideas above. There are no hard and fast rules that apply to all nonprofits!

Now that we've covered a direct method of communications in email, let's turn our attention to an indirect method: social media.

Part V

SOCIAL MEDIA

Social media is an undeniably significant and nearly irrevocable part of the modern marketing toolkit. It is also one that confounds not just the nonprofit sector, but marketers of every industry worldwide.

Why is this?

Similar to search engine optimization, making the most of social media relies on manipulating your content in a way that pleases the algorithms that control what gets seen on platforms like Facebook, Twitter, and Instagram.

However, it wasn't always this way.

In the early days of social media, content was typically shown chronologically to any user who had opted-in to see it. If you liked a page on Facebook, you'd see all of its posts as soon as they happened.

Now, newsfeed content is displayed algorithmically, in a sort of meritocratic way. Generally, the more engagement a post receives, the more it gets seen (a catch-22 for sure and one that we'll dive deeper into later). More recently, that engagement requirement can be augmented or sidestepped altogether through paid advertising on the major platforms. For example, you can "boost" a post or create a paid ad to gain higher newsfeed visibility.

For nonprofits, these changes have been somewhat traumatic and frustrating.

We aren't alone. The for-profit world is frustrated too.

Author and speaker Scott Stratten's response to the ocean of consternation over Facebook's monetization strategy went viral, as did a post from video blogger Derek Muller of Veritasium. Both represent damning indictments of Facebook's advertising model.

And yet, Facebook continues to be something that nonprofits obsess over, as if firing off a status update on a daily basis is going to result in a wave of donations. Combined with privacy concerns, data breaches, and declining overall usage, it's hard to blame any brand marketer from abandoning the network altogether.

Before we jump into ways that you can avoid being robotic on social media, while also working with the robots who control what is seen and not seen in the social communities, let's first evaluate why we're on social media and whether it's a good idea to begin with.

CHAPTER 24

Digital Sharecropping in the Social Media Age

Did you know that nonprofits raised billions of dollars before the advent of Facebook?

It's true! It is still possible to run a successful fundraising operation without 100% organic post visibility. Really!

And if you're mad that people used to be able to see more of your content than they do now, let me just say this: Get over it. Facebook doesn't owe you anything. You've been renting space on land you don't own—be wary of digital sharecropping.

Quite simply, *digital sharecropping* is the act of using a third-party platform to publicize your brand. Your brand creates the content and publishes it on an external platform in exchange for exposure on that platform, similar to how sharecroppers would tend land owned by someone else in exchange for a share of the yield. The tenants do all the work while the landowner reaps a majority of the benefits.

159

Sonia Simone of Copyblogger calls digital sharecropping "the most dangerous threat to your online marketing" and with good reason. Given the recent and constant algorithmic changes on Facebook and Google, it can be very risky to place all of your eggs in someone else's basket.

Nowhere is the nonprofit sector's martyr complex more evident than in the comment sections of frequently published blogs and articles about Facebook making changes to its News Feed algorithm: "This hurts nonprofits!" "It isn't fair, Mark Zuckerberg!" "Why won't you help nonprofits?"

But I'm not here to bash Facebook. I'm here to say that it's time for nonprofits to stop making Facebook out to be the villain.

Forrester Research recommends that marketers shouldn't "dedicate a paid ad budget to Facebook."

Furthermore, studies show that usage among teens is slipping, while tweens are skipping the network entirely in favor of Instagram, Snapchat, and Twitter. Pew Research reported that 61% of current Facebook users admitted to having voluntarily taken a break from using Facebook for a period of several weeks or more.

We haven't even gotten into data privacy.

Consider the following: Facebook might not be the best channel for acquiring new donors or stewarding current ones. The expectation that mounds of cash will roll in after only exerting a minimal effort to click a few buttons on Facebook may be disproportionate to reality.

Sure, there is a ton of data and case studies that show nonprofits can raise a lot of money on Facebook. That's great! But planning and deploying paid advertisements and boosted post campaigns shouldn't be taken lightly.

Have you ever created an ad or boosted a post on Facebook? It's not easy.

Let's say you were gifted a grant. Where would you begin? These are just a few examples of what goes into a Facebook ad: Ad Type, Page Post Engagement, Page Likes, Clicks to Website, Website Conversions, App Installs, App Engagement, Event Responses, Offer Claims, Campaign Duration, Schedule, Budget per day, Campaign Cost, Price Bid Per Impression, Price Bid Per Click, Demographic (Target Audience), Location, Age, Gender, Language, Relationship Status, Interests.

Easy-peasy, right? You'll also need to write copy for the ad, source an image, and optimize both the copy and image for conversions. Also, don't forget, you have to create a campaign, landing page, or call to action to promote—along with goals and objectives—before you can even dig into this.

Midsize and enterprise for-profit brands have entire teams within their marketing departments solely dedicated to paid search, social media ads, and retargeting. It is an exact science with little room for error, but a lot of room for A/B testing and conversion rate optimization. These marketers live and die by single-cent changes (yes, as in pennies) in cost-per-impression and cost-per-click. It often takes numerous campaigns to discover what works and what doesn't.

Even if a nonprofit staffer at a small- or medium-sized organization could find the time and garner the expertise to adequately plan and deploy an ad or sponsored post, it's likely that time would be better invested elsewhere. I don't mean to discourage anyone reading this, but I wouldn't be terribly excited about receiving a brand-new BMW if told I had to rebuild the engine myself to drive it.

Instead, let's focus on the personal touch as often as possible:

- Phone calls make a personal connection with a supporter.
- Handwritten notes make a supporter feel special, apropos of nothing.
- Email consistently beats all other digital channels in engagement.

Here are just a few things I would prioritize higher than creating and publishing Facebook content:

- Email your donors whatever it is you want them to know.
- Call donors to say thank you.
- Write handwritten notes to donors.
- Survey first-time donors.
- Give tours to first-time donors (if tours are applicable to your organization).
- Take a walk through the forest and contemplate your own mortality.

Yes, all of this might take longer. Yes, all of this might seem like a chore. But the dividends these tasks will pay will far exceed any results that the average nonprofit can achieve through Facebook.

Let's all stop acting so helpless, and instead, be empowered to communicate with our constituents in more personal and meaningful ways.

CHAPTER 25

Examining the Facebook Algorithm

Yes, you can overcome the algorithm by throwing money at Facebook in the form of boosted posts and ads. And yes, this probably means that the deck is stacked against nonprofits due to limited resources.

But you *can* also overcome the algorithm with engaging, interesting, emotional, personal, and authentic content. You *can* overcome the algorithm by not posting random boring, promotional, and impersonal content.

In a very general sense, Facebook's algorithm operates similarly to Google's: It favors content that users find valuable. Valuable content often includes

- posts with lots of comments
- posts with lots of likes
- post types that users seem to prefer more than others (e.g., photo, video, or status update)

- posts that receive a high volume of likes, comments, or shares in a short time
- posts that tag other pages within the text
- posts that are liked or commented on by one's friends
- posts from pages that one interacts with often

In early 2018, Facebook announced a sweeping change that favors content from individuals above content from brands and businesses:

> *Recently we've gotten feedback from our community that public content—posts from businesses, brands and media—is crowding out the personal moments that lead us to connect more with each other.*
>
> *Based on this, we're making a major change to how we build Facebook. I'm changing the goal I give our product teams from focusing on helping you find relevant content to helping you have more meaningful social interactions.*
>
> *We started making changes in this direction last year, but it will take months for this new focus to make its way through all our products. The first changes you'll see will be in News Feed, where you can expect to see more from your friends, family and groups.*
>
> *As we roll this out, you'll see less public content like posts from businesses, brands, and media. And the public content you see more will be held to the same standard—it should encourage meaningful interactions between people.*
>
> *At its best, Facebook has always been about personal connections. By focusing on bringing people closer together— whether it's with family and friends, or around important*

moments in the world—we can help make sure that Facebook is time well spent.

Many brand marketers, including those at nonprofits, panicked at the announcement. Even though News Feed visibility had been declining for years, this felt like a deathblow.

However, I believe that nonprofits stand to benefit from this change. Given that philanthropy is a deeply personal act, nonprofits have the ability to tap into a pre-existing inclination for individuals to use social media to promote the causes they care about.

In other words, your supporters are your most powerful tool, not your brand account.

CHAPTER 26

The "Three A's" of a Winning Social Media Content Strategy

The most common piece of advice found in the wake of frequent social network algorithm updates is some variation of "post good, engaging content and you'll be fine!"

It's true that the quality of your content is a major factor in how well it performs, algorithms aside. Even though "good content" might not be enough to overcome the newest change, it's never a bad exercise to evaluate what you're posting to Facebook and why.

One of my favorite frameworks for nonprofit social media content is the "Three A's"—Appreciation, Advocacy, and Appeals.

If you aren't using Facebook (and really any social network) to . . .

- show appreciation to your donors (appreciation),
- tell stories of who your organization is helping (advocacy), and
- ask for help in a social way (appeals),

167

. . . you likely won't get much engagement, even if your posts have 100% organic visibility.

Let's dive into each of the Three A's, beginning with the most important, Appreciation.

Appreciation

A primary focus of your brand's social media accounts should be donor appreciation.

Historically, donors could only be acknowledged through offline means: a phone call, a thank-you letter, or recognition at a live event. Social media allows for high-impact, low-cost public recognition that, when deployed strategically, can create stickiness between your organization and its supporters while generating new exposure. It's also an excellent way to shift away from broadcasting and drive engagement.

By putting donors on display, you allow them to publicize their philanthropy. Donors feel good when they support a cause they believe in, and they feel even better when everyone knows it. Tagging users in posts, photos, and tweets taps into social media users' natural inclinations toward exhibitionism. Not only are you showing your appreciation, but you're increasing the chances that your supporters will share and retweet information about your organization.

It is important to showcase your followers and to show your appreciation for them. However, you don't want to annoy your diverse collection of followers by only posting donor-centric content. On platforms like Facebook, where you might post only once or twice a day, consider using posts such as "Donor of the Day" or "Donor of the Week" to highlight supporters and why they give in a way that breaks that content out from other posts.

So that you can more easily highlight supporters, don't be afraid to ask for Twitter usernames or other social handles and store them with other contact information in your donor database.

Donors aren't the only supporters you can recognize publicly on social media. Employees, volunteers, and vendors are all excellent candidates for public recognition and appreciation. After all, your charity will not function without them.

Now to the second A for Advocacy.

Advocacy

Every nonprofit has a mission and cause for which they advocate. Social media is an excellent platform for telling followers about all the good work your organization is doing, while putting the spotlight on donors who make it possible.

Remember that in the DonorVoice donor loyalty research, "impactful storytelling" represented three of the top seven reasons why donors keep giving to a nonprofit.

1. **Donor perceives your organization to be effective in trying to achieve its mission.**
2. Donor knows what to expect from your organization with each interaction.
3. Donor receives a timely thank-you.
4. Donor receives opportunities to make his or her views known.
5. **Donor is given the feeling that he or she is part of an important cause.**
6. Donor feels his or her involvement is appreciated.
7. **Donor receives information showing who is being helped.**

You are likely already telling these stories in your newsletter, appeals, and other communications. Why not social media?

For example, The Innocence Project, which helps exonerate the wrongly convicted through DNA testing and criminal justice reforms, posts touching moments in the lives of those who they have freed, like the first trip to a shopping mall to buy their first non-prison clothing in years.

Agapé Therapeutic Riding Resources shows off photos of their guests, like special needs children or recovering drug addicts, who are able to receive therapy through their services. These types of visual posts show how the therapy works and that the organization is fulfilling its mission.

Outside the Box, which provides job training, has a regular "Feel Good Friday" post to show photographs of guests enjoying their time at their facility. It's a simple visual reminder of how they are serving the community.

Follow other groups that advocate for or conduct research into the topics that are relevant to your nonprofit and share their content. Getting involved with their content—which can be done by engaging in discussions, asking questions, and sharing stories—can go a long way in boosting awareness of your own cause and organization.

While sharing content from others, don't forget to look inside your own organization. Publish the knowledge that your staff holds in the form of blog posts, videos, podcasts, and webinars, and share it via social media.

On to the third A for Appeals.

Appeals

No one will deny that social media has been a game-changer for online fundraising. There's no reason not to solicit donations directly from Twitter, Facebook, and the like, provided your appeals occur proportionately to other forms of content.

The more specific you can be in an appeal, the better. For example, a tweet asking for donations of a specific item due to a shortage performs much better than a generic "please consider donating today." Donors like to know where their money is going, so don't forget to share stories of donation impact.

You also should not forget you don't have to do it alone. By leveraging Influencers, you can increase your promotional reach exponentially. Include high-visibility donors in planning and deploying social media campaigns. Ask board members, volunteers, and employees to include your organization in their profiles and bios. Make your brand part of their personal brand!

It's no accident that this is listed third on the list. Internet users are becoming more and more aware of when they are being solicited and advertised to. Concurrently, marketers and fundraisers are always looking for new digital methods of new customer and donor acquisition.

This is a volatile combination. When you shift away from solicitation as a primary focus of social media usage, you can begin to build an authentic community around your brand. A balanced approach to the "Three A's" and the rule of thirds can set your nonprofit organization up for social media success.

Stop doing somersaults to get around the algorithm—or worse, spending hours researching what tricks can get you around the algorithm—and embrace being social (being human!) on social media.

CHAPTER 27

LinkedIn –
The Undervalued Secret Weapon

While not the sexiest of social networks, LinkedIn offers a variety of ways to promote your nonprofit, if you're savvy enough to take advantage of them.

After all, think of all the ways that employees and employers engage with nonprofits:

- corporate volunteerism
- individual volunteerism
- matching gifts
- board and committee membership
- nonprofit employer brand

To that end, here are a few ways you can leverage LinkedIn.

Get your organizational leaders invested in writing and publishing blog posts. In 2014, LinkedIn opened up their publishing platform to all users. Previously, it was reserved only for 500 or so "Influencers." Now, anyone can publish a blog post to LinkedIn's network of millions of users.

Blogging on LinkedIn is a nice supplement (or alternative) to blogging on your nonprofit's website. Posts get wide visibility right away because of LinkedIn's built-in network, as opposed to having to promote your own hosted blog posts.

Given the professional nature of the network, your executive director is well-suited to write about hiring, volunteer management, the financial and administrative side of running a nonprofit, and other "business-oriented" topics. Posts that offer tips and lessons learned often perform better than promotional posts.

Ask your supporters to include your nonprofit organization in their "Volunteer Experience & Causes" profile section. You don't get what you don't ask for. Encourage board members, committee members, volunteers, and other long-term supporters to add your organization to the "Volunteer Experience & Causes" section of their profiles.

If you have a company page, the listing will connect to it. It's a great way to show off your organization and asking your supporters to add to their profiles is a nice form of recognition. When added, it will be posted to the public News Feed. These posts typically generate lots of likes and "Congratulations!" comments, which furthers your organization's exposure.

Be sure your employees employment history connects to your organization's corporate page. A common mistake I see often on LinkedIn profiles is not connecting your job listing to the company page of the organization you work for. When adding or editing a job listing, first begin typing the name of the organization you work for. LinkedIn will auto-populate possible organizations it has pages for. Be sure to select one of these options, rather than just typing in the name of your organization and creating the listing.

When done correctly, you should be able to click through to the organization page. When done incorrectly, a click will bring you to a search results page that shows other people employed by the organization. You want to send people to your page instead!

Have employees add media content to their job listing. If your nonprofit has a corporate overview video, you can have your employees add it to their job listing on their profiles. You can also add other media files, allowing people to learn more about the organization right from the profile.

Have board members connect with leadership at companies who support you. Board members are excellent ambassadors for your organization. If they themselves are also business professionals, it's not a stretch to ask them to connect with leaders at other businesses who support you.

The CEOs of organizations who are your sponsors or vendors or who offer matching gift opportunities or send employees to volunteer are excellent prospects for this kind of outreach.

It may not be known at the top levels of the organization that this kind of support is happening, so reaching out to connect and saying thank you for that support offers a double whammy. If that support is known, the appreciation will be appreciated! Plus, CEOs will be connected for the foreseeable future, creating "stickiness" between the two brands and allowing for future posts and content to be seen.

CHAPTER 28

The Art of Social Listening

The consensus among social media practitioners is that only a portion of your messaging should be promotional. For example, "the rule of thirds" states that only 33% of your content should be promotional, while "the 80/20 rule" limits it to just 20%. It makes sense, doesn't it? After all, who among us wants to be constantly solicited to on social media?

So, if the majority of your social media postings should be conversational, how do you go about generating those interactions? The key is listening. Listening is the ideal starting point to engaging new and prospective followers in a meaningful conversation.

You Can't Broadcast Until You Have a Community

If you're boasting only single or double-digit follower counts on your active social networks, your posts are the equivalent of shouting into a void, especially when you consider that algorithm-controlled networks (like Facebook and Instagram) limit the visibility of your posts to only about 10% of your followers. Shouting into a void isn't the best way to gain followers.

One of the best ways (though not the only way) to gain followers is to monitor ongoing conversations and engage with them if it makes sense to do so. Listen for mentions of your brand name, your cause, your events, or any other topic that is on-brand for you.

Listening Gives You an Authentic Reason to Engage

Savvy nonprofit marketers will identify social media users in their community who are either influential or in a position to help (geographically close, civically engaged, etc.) or both.

Unfortunately, there is a tendency to simply spam these people by bulk-tweeting to them or tagging them in promotional posts. It's no surprise that these messages are often ignored. Social media is not the same as mass email marketing.

Once you have identified those you want to have a conversation with (either through listening or direct research), engage them individually either around a conversation already in progress or by initiating a new one that is unique to just them. This kind of interaction is much more authentic than blasting out the same message to a large group of people and hoping one or two responds.

Broadcasting En Masse is Not Effective

If you are using a tool that lets you schedule and distribute content en masse to multiple social media networks at once, you may want to reconsider.

Sending the same update to all of your networks at the same time is universally regarded as a bad idea. Each social network has its own unique community, style, and cadence expectations. It's also counter-intuitive to the whole idea of being "social." When you're at a party, do you go up and talk to people individually or do you shout from the corner of the room and hope someone hears you?

Be sure you are regularly monitoring the conversation not just around your brand but around the topics or issues your nonprofit is engaged in. Hashtags, public posts, and group discussions are an excellent place to mine ideas for content that will hit the mark.

This brings up an interesting question. Should you or your employees accept a friend request from a donor on Facebook? Should you send a friend request yourself? Let's explore both sides of the argument.

The Case for Becoming Facebook Friends with Donors

As a fundraiser, your job is to build relationships with donors. Sure, you can get by with one-off gifts from people you never truly get to know on a more personal level, but it's not a path to sustainability.

While there's no replacement for in-person interactions, and as impersonal as social media can be sometimes, Facebook can still be an amazing way to go beyond a transactional relationship.

Imagine the power of all the information you can glean from someone's profile and regular status updates, like sending a note of congratulations or condolence when something major happens in their life, or being able to tailor appeals to them based on what you learn about their interests and passions. You might even be able to infer why giving suddenly stopped.

Besides that, there's an opportunity for direct interaction that you can't quite get through email or direct mail. At the very least, you can say thank you. Most donors love to put their philanthropy on display, and when you're connected with someone directly on Facebook, it's much easier to tag them in posts, photos and videos— and get them to share the content published from your brand page.

Maybe you're reading my case for friendship and thinking, "That sounds a little creepy, Steven!" It's possible that you might alienate a donor by weaponizing too much of their personal information, but consider this: If they initiate the connection, aren't they opening the door to it?

And what do you risk by not accepting a request from a funder? Couldn't that alienate them? Now, if you initiate the connection and put all the info to use, that's a different story...

The Case against Becoming Facebook Friends with Donors

All of the benefits above may not be worth the risk of screwing up a good thing! There's always a risk of alienating someone (or being alienated) when you open up the more personal aspects of your life to others.

Imagine friending a donor only to have them turned off by your posts (politics comes to mind, but heck, they might even hate your favorite sports team—who knows?) or vice versa. It might become harder to do your job if you're constantly thinking to yourself, "Ugh, I have to meet with that (conservative or progressive) today."

Sure, professional maturity should prevail, but we are human after all. So why even open the door to all of this when there are other relationship-building channels that are more effective?

If you're worried that your posts on Facebook might alienate potential donors, it might be time to rethink what you're posting and why. Even though Facebook is somewhat of a closed system, other social networks are not, and if a funder wanted to see what you're posting, they could do it pretty easily. It's naive to think that you can keep your personal digital life completely separate from your professional one.

Lastly, if you're going to open the door to nonprofit employees connecting with people on social media, you're going to need a documented social media policy. After all, they are representing the organization.

Now that you've optimized your automated and semi-automated digital toolkit to be more human, let's look at how to deploy them together in the context of a unified campaign.

Part VI

GIVING TUESDAY

If you've made it this far in the book, it probably won't surprise you to learn that I'm not the biggest fan of Giving Tuesday. Giving Tuesday has grown so big, so fast since its inception that its gravitational pull seems to impact the entire final two months of the fundraising year.

However, it has become one of my favorite days to study the behaviors and tactics of nonprofits who are attempting to capitalize on the philanthropic bonanza. It's the one day a year where all the dangers previously outlined in this book coalesce and culminate in the most robotic and impersonal single day of fundraising from the donor's point of view.

In 2016, I chronicled 25 "secret shopping" donations on Giving Tuesday, similar to my $5 experiments. In 2016 and 2017, I did an analysis of the email appeals I received. In 2018, I made a one-time gift to all 10 of the nonprofits I give to monthly to see if they would recognize my "extra" gift on Giving Tuesday.

For my 2016 gifts, the results were similar to—or arguably slightly worse than—my other $5 experiments. Out of 25 gifts, only one nonprofit made a thank-you phone call, while only seven hand-signed their thank-you letter. Five nonprofits asked me for a second gift within 14 days, including one who asked me in their thank-you letter.

In 2016 and 2017, the email appeals I received showed a high disregard for all of the advice in this book.

- A majority of these appeals reference "Giving Tuesday" in the subject line.
- Few that did also explained what it is in the email body.
- Most emails were sent before Noon Eastern.
- Most organizations only sent one email appeal on Giving Tuesday.

Because the emails I received lacked personalization (referencing donor type or asking for a specific amount), it is safe to assume that these Giving Tuesday campaigns were not segmented. In fact, one organization's second appeal includes the following: "If you have already made a gift today, THANK YOU! If not, it's not too late!"

Compared to 2016, a much higher percentage of organizations directed email recipients to a native donation page, rather than an off-site hosted, third-party page. This suggests that more nonprofits are adopting conversion rate optimization techniques for online giving, which is a positive.

Organizations who sent multiple emails were aggressive in pushing a matching deadline or a donation shortfall. The subject lines became increasingly desperate with each subsequent email. Most organizations found little reason to ask for money other than the fact that it was Giving Tuesday. In 2018, when I made an extra "13th" gift to organizations where I was a monthly donor, virtually none of them recognized my extra gift on Giving Tuesday.

With the amount of time and energy spent on Giving Tuesday, not to mention the impact that it can have on year-end fundraising results, a real opportunity exists to optimize and humanize all of your digital fundraising efforts to capitalize on this online day of giving.

The significance of Giving Tuesday may also give you the push you need to convince leadership that these changes are essential. The best part? You can reap the benefits all year long!

CHAPTER 29

Preparing for and Standing Out on Giving Tuesday

M uch like any fundraising campaign, jumping in without a clear plan of action is a great way to ensure failure. Giving Tuesday carries with it unique challenges. It's a day when inboxes are saturated, and servers are pushed to the breaking point.

There's no shortage of advice on Giving Tuesday messaging, design, and targeting. So, allow me instead to challenge the premise that you have to fundraise on Giving Tuesday.

On Giving Tuesday 2017, I received 86 emails from over 60 organizations. Eighty-three of the 86 were solicitations. Of those, three stood out to me. Perhaps these organizations recognized that most nonprofits would be seeking donations. So, they instead took a different approach.

1. YMCA of Greater Omaha's Ask: Volunteer Request

Out of 86 emails, this was the only volunteer request I received, which means it likely stood out with other donors too. In the email, they equated volunteering with "giving the gift of joy to a child," instantly connecting the volunteer and the organization's service recipients.

2. Humanitri's Ask: Social Media Sharing

Similar to the YMCA of Greater Omaha, Humanitri also asked for email recipients to share on social media why they support the organization. The ask goes beyond just Facebook, and the email recipients were given ideas to craft their post.

3. charity: water's Ask: Personal Fundraising

The Giving Tuesday email from charity: water encouraged you to share a link to a personal fundraising page, so that you could go out and raise money for them, rather than (or in addition to) donating yourself.

Yes, this obviously requires a substantial investment in the technology, but conceptually, asking your supporters to raise money for you on a day saturated with messaging from brands seems like a good idea.

Another strategy that seems to be gaining popularity is turning Giving Tuesday into Thanking Tuesday—a day for donor stewardship. Eschewing a monetary ask is definitely a risky proposition on Giving Tuesday, but one that might make you stand out from the crowd.

Should you decide to use Giving Tuesday as a day of traditional fundraising, there is one extremely practical task that all nonprofits should do before Giving Tuesday to help ensure the day goes off without a hitch: Test your donation forms.

Test Your Donation Forms

It may seem silly but checking your donation form(s) to ensure they are working properly is a very prudent task to complete before Giving Tuesday. Remember, Giving Tuesday is a day of online giving, and if your donation form(s) isn't working, or the post-donation process isn't quite up-to-snuff, you could have a big problem. Potential donors could get stuck during the donation process.

Go secret shopping by donating to your own nonprofit through your website. Here are some things to look for:

- Is it easy for website visitors to find your donation page?
- Does the donation page load on all browsers and devices (especially mobile)?
- Does the donation form also load?
- Can you fill out the donation form and complete the process with no problems? Run an actual credit card to be sure!
- Does the confirmation page load correctly?
- Are you pleased with the content of the confirmation page?
- Is the email confirmation sent right away?
- Are you pleased with the content of the email confirmation?
- Is the transaction entered into your donor database automatically?
- Is that transaction information correct?

It's not the most exciting task in the world but testing now can save you a lot of heartache later. Don't let half of Giving Tuesday pass you by before discovering that your online donation forms aren't working!

CHAPTER 30

Writing Email Subject Lines for Giving Tuesday

An email subject line serves one purpose: to get the recipient to open the email.

No pressure, right?

When it comes to sending Giving Tuesday email appeals specifically, there are two words you should absolutely avoid including in the subject line: Giving Tuesday.

Why? Because these two words are the most frequently used words in Giving Tuesday email appeal subject lines. And if you use them, you won't stand out.

In 2016, I received 40 email appeals on Giving Tuesday. Twenty-seven of them contained either "Giving Tuesday" or "#GivingTuesday" with most of them saying some variation of, "It's Giving Tuesday" or "Support (organization name) on Giving Tuesday."

The exceptions alluded to Giving Tuesday—for instance, "Today is the day…" or "Only 4 hours left to give!"

Assuming that the average person encounters and subscribes to several nonprofits throughout the year, it's fair to assume that their inboxes on Giving Tuesday are inundated with subject lines that all say pretty much the same thing.

Fatigue and annoyance are going to set in quickly . . . Allow me to give a shout-out to the organization who sent me an email with a subject line stating, "We know you've gotten a lot of emails today."

The other reason to avoid frequently used subject line appeals is that you shift the purpose to give away from impact and toward an arbitrary date to give. This makes the appeal organization-centric and not donor-centric (it's your timeline, not theirs).

Very few of the examples above allude to the impact of a gift or the purpose of the campaign, such as an item or project they are raising money for. Thus, they don't do much to move me toward action. A matching challenge may be the only justifiable reason for using Giving Tuesday in the subject line.

To Hashtag or Not to Hashtag

You probably noticed that many of the 40 subject lines above format Giving Tuesday as "#GivingTuesday."

In my opinion, there's not much point in using a hashtag in an email subject line, since the point of a hashtag is for it to be clicked to see all the other messages, posts, and tweets about that topic. If some of your email recipients aren't familiar with Giving Tuesday, seeing "#GivingTuesday" may further confuse them. You might also consider not using "#GivingTuesday" in your social media posts, since, when clicked, it will just bring up a giant list of other nonprofits making appeals.

CHAPTER 31

Giving Tuesday and Monthly Donors

One of the most common concerns around Giving Tuesday is the fear that it will cannibalize year-end giving. This is certainly a fair question, given the timing of the event. In other words, if we put a ton of time and energy into a campaign in late November or early December, will donors consider a Giving Tuesday gift to be their year-end gift, instead of giving something extra to our appeal?

Of course, proponents of Giving Tuesday, particularly technology vendors with a vested interest, maintain that there is no evidence that Giving Tuesday cannibalizes year-end giving. This very well may be true. Despite Giving Tuesday's growth in popularity, it is still dwarfed by giving on New Year's Eve.

It would be a shame to miss out on all of the philanthropic energy that Giving Tuesday generates just because you were worried about donor fatigue.

Jeff Schreifels of the Veritus Group, one of my favorite writers and speakers in the philanthropy world, reminds us that, "Asking your donors to make an investment in your organization that will make an impact on the world is one the greatest things you can do for a donor. Donors want to give. They need to give. Donors experience joy in their lives when they give their money away."

All of this being said, there is a unique group of donors that deserves special attention on Giving Tuesday so that they won't be alienated by your efforts.

Experiment: How Should Nonprofits Treat Monthly Donors on Giving Tuesday?

Monthly donors are a unique group of donors, so any and all appeals sent to them should be handled with a little caution. Consider this:

- They trust you enough to give you their payment information for an automatic withdrawal.
- Their retention rates are typically above 90%.
- Their lifetime value is high, even if the individual donation amount is small.

Giving Tuesday, in particular, represents a unique opportunity to annoy monthly donors.

- "I'm already giving 12 times a year. You're asking me again?"
- "I'm already giving 12 times a year. I just gave the other day!"

Don't get me wrong. I think monthly donors should be asked for stand-alone gifts throughout the year, but not in a one-size-fits-all way on Giving Tuesday. In fact, I think Giving Tuesday represents an extraordinary opportunity to steward monthly donors and get a "bonus" gift!

But do most nonprofits think that way?

In 2018, I ran a little experiment. I made a one-time gift to all 10 of the nonprofits I give to monthly, whether or not they asked me to. The amount I gave was the same as the monthly recurring gift, so if I normally gave $50 a month, I gave $50 on Giving Tuesday. This constitutes a "13th" gift to the nonprofit.

In doing so, I was looking for a few things to happen:

- Would they acknowledge it as a Giving Tuesday gift?
- Would they acknowledge me as a monthly donor?
- Would they acknowledge my gift as an "extra" donation for the year?

I was also curious to see how nonprofits would communicate to me leading up to and on the day of Giving Tuesday. In other words, would they segment communications to me as a monthly donor and make special appeals to me, or would they steward me in a unique way?

Here are the organizations I gave to, and how much:

1. local adult day center: $50
2. local public radio: $5
3. local chapter of national social service: $10
4. local social service (aging and disability solutions): $10
5. local social service (child advocacy): $10
6. local social service (teen homelessness): $25
7. local social service (refugee resettlement): $25
8. non-local conservation agency: $10
9. national gun rights advocacy: $11
10. charity: water: $10

Just in case you're thinking, "Those are pretty small gifts. Do you really expect the red-carpet treatment?"—consider the lifetime value (assuming a 10% attrition rate for monthly donors):

- A $50 per month donor has a lifetime value of $6,000.
- A $5 per month donor has a lifetime value of $600.
- A $10 per month donor has a lifetime value of $1,200.

And that's without any additional gifts!

So, what happened? Only two organizations communicated to me in the seven days leading up to Giving Tuesday (11/27). I got a Giving Tuesday appeal on 11/24 from the teen homelessness organization and a Happy Thanksgiving email on 11/21 from the refugee resettlement organization.

Now, let's look at what each organization sent to me on Giving Tuesday. For these, I would have expected a couple of things:

- addressing me as a monthly donor
- asking for a Giving Tuesday gift or mentioning Giving Tuesday
- some sort of acknowledgment that this is an "extra" gift beyond my monthly contribution

Most did none of these things.

The local public radio station emailed me, did not greet me as a monthly donor, asked for a Giving Tuesday gift, and asked me to start a monthly commitment (which, of course, I had already done). The national gun rights advocacy group did the same.

Only charity: water did something that appeared segmented. They sent me one email on Giving Tuesday, addressed me as a monthly donor, and simply thanked me for being one.

So, let's look at the charity: water email, since it was obviously a standout in the experiment:

Subject: We're inspired by your generosity.

Seven years ago, #GivingTuesday was brand new—just a scrappy idea started by our friends at the 92nd Street Y in

New York City. Then, generous people just like you stepped in, and that scrappy idea began to spread.

Today, millions of people around the world will celebrate generosity by giving their time, money, and voices to support the organizations they love. They'll counter problems like dirty water, poverty, education, and homelessness. And the world will be better for it.

We want to thank you.

Not just for being part of #GivingTuesday today, but for changing lives every month as a member of The Spring and inspiring generosity in the people around you too.

#GivingTuesday is a perfect picture of the world we believe in, thanks to supporters like you. And today is going to be another beautiful day.

In this letter, there is no ask at all, just pure stewardship that acknowledges me as a monthly donor.

The nonprofit also sent a second email later that morning (also without an ask) explaining how one of their water filtration systems works, with a thank-you for support at the end.

So, what should have happened with all the rest? Should nonprofits filter out their monthly donors from Giving Tuesday communications? No.

I understand the mentality here: Maybe you don't want to bug donors or mess with a good thing. But it's a great opportunity to fund a specific project, communicate the impact of their monthly donations (and increase that impact), or let them know you specifically aren't asking them, and instead thanking them. Giving Tuesday doesn't have to be exclusively Asking Tuesday.

Should nonprofits communicate to their monthly donors in the days leading up to Giving Tuesday? I say yes. Research shows that "priming the pump" leading up to an appeal is very effective.

Should nonprofits send a segmented appeal to their monthly donors on Giving Tuesday? Yes, again. Monthly donors should get a unique appeal that no other segment of donors gets. Consider starting the appeal off by saying, "You're already a monthly donor making a huge impact, and for that, we're so grateful."

I find it so interesting that all but two of the other nonprofit organizations did not send me an email appeal on Giving Tuesday. Perhaps I was simply filtered out because I am a monthly donor? That's a missed opportunity.

Should nonprofits thank monthly donors who give on Giving Tuesday with a segmented acknowledgment? Yes, I believe this is a no-brainer. It's a big deal for a monthly donor to make an "extra" gift, so act accordingly!

On to Giving Tuesday follow-up.

CHAPTER 32

Giving Tuesday Follow-Up Segmentation

My experiment didn't end with examining the appeals. I also donated to all 10 organizations on Giving Tuesday, just to see how they would follow up.

None of the thank-yous I received via email or snail mail acknowledged that I was a monthly donor who made an "extra" donation on Giving Tuesday. I did receive one handwritten note, which was very nice, but no thank-you phone calls. All but one organization sent me a letter in the mail, and one of those nine had an appeal reach me before the formal thank-you letter. Most of the letters did mention that it was a Giving Tuesday gift, though, suggesting a level of segmentation. All included a handwritten signature with a little P.S. note.

It's important to remember that the sun rising on the morning after Giving Tuesday doesn't mean your work is done. If you plan on retaining those dollars and donors, the real work is about to begin. Your ability to retain new and returning donors that gave on Giving Tuesday will be the true measure of whether your campaign was successful or not.

One of the worst things your organization can do is to lump all of these donors into a standard, one-size-fits-all acknowledgment. Because Giving Tuesday is so unique and isolated, segmentation and personalized follow-up is an absolute must.

Here are several ways to segment your Giving Tuesday donors. These segments are broken into two groups: those who gave at or below your average gift amount, and those who gave above your average gift amount. This is especially helpful for nonprofits with high gift volumes where it may be difficult to get into detailed segmenting. You can concentrate on those who give above average amounts. If you don't have a high gift volume, consider ignoring the gift amount.

1. First-Time Donors via Giving Tuesday-At or Below Your Average Gift Amount

This is a critical group given what an opportunity Giving Tuesday represents for new donor acquisition.

These folks may have just recently discovered your organization and are in the greatest need of stewarding. You might want to find out what compelled them to give to your organization for the first time. It's also critical that you communicate the impact that their donations make.

Suggested action: a phone call from an executive or board member.

As many first-time donors as possible should receive a phone call. Don't let this group churn and burn, or you may experience negative ROI on your Giving Tuesday efforts as a whole.

2. Repeat Donors via Giving Tuesday (Only Donation This Year)–At or Below Your Average Gift Amount

These folks have given to you before, but for some reason waited until Giving Tuesday to give this year. Try to find out why.

Suggested action: send a donor survey.

As Roger Craver of *The Agitator* often states, a donor survey is a great way to measure donor commitment. Even if donors do not complete the survey, merely receiving one will make a positive impression.

3. Repeat Donors via Giving Tuesday (Repeat Donation This Year)–At or Below Your Average Gift Amount

These folks probably think you're great. They're your most loyal donors – keep them that way. The biggest danger here is letting the Giving Tuesday gift go unnoticed among their other gifts that year. Treat the Giving Tuesday gift just as special as if it was a first-time or major gift.

Suggested action: since this (hopefully) won't be the only thank-you they've received from you, do something fun or off-the-wall, like a handwritten note, photo, or a quick video.

4. Donors on Giving Tuesday–Above Your Average Gift Amount

These donors could be first-time or repeat donors, but they gave above your average gift amount on Giving Tuesday. Treat them according to the classifications above, but with consideration given to the larger than average gifts. For repeat donors, look to see if the gift represents an upgrade over their previous gift(s). If so, these donors might be ripe for a major gift or bequest conversation. Giving Tuesday can offer a wealth of insight!

Part VII

CRYSTAL BALL – FUTURE PREDICTIONS AND WHAT TO LOOK OUT FOR

W e've spent a lot of time on advice for dealing with the current fundraising technology landscape, so I want to spend these closing pages looking at technology that exists but isn't quite as ubiquitous. I think that these channels of communication will have much greater prominence in our tech stacks—the common sets of programs we use—than they currently do.

CHAPTER 33

A Multi-Channel Renaissance

Let's turn our attention to analog communications and how they can work in tandem with your digital stack.

Yes, analog and digital can work together!

First, it's important to agree to this premise: There is room for a robust communications strategy that includes both social media and handwritten notes. Or an acknowledgment strategy that includes email and phone calls. Or an acquisition strategy that involves in-person events and AI-driven prospect research.

Too often organizations take a binary approach. "We're all digital," or "We're old school; we haven't entered the digital age." Neither is wrong, but you don't have to choose one or the other. Phone calls and handwritten notes don't have to evolve into an exclusive use of email and social media.

Likewise, you don't have to swing the pendulum back to all-analog, just because of a perceived oversaturation of the digital inbox. Keep in mind that a donor may see something online and choose to act by mailing you a check. Conversely, they may make an online gift after receiving a direct mail piece.

As such, there's no reason why you should lock yourself into a donor communications channel that mirrors the gift acquisition channel. Not only are you assuming that their preferred giving channel was how they were acquired, but you're also assuming a communication preference that may not have yet been stated. You also risk using a communications channel that may be less effective than another.

According to Network for Good's "Our Digital Dilemma" study, nonprofits using multi-channel communications that switch to one single channel saw a year-over-year retention drop of 31.32%. Conversely, nonprofits that increased the number of donor engagement channels (from 1 to 2 or more) retained 11.89% more donors year over year.

And it makes sense, doesn't it? Few of us practice channel exclusivity in our lives. We read mail, email, texts, and tweets. We watch videos and listen to podcasts. We consume media in multiple formats before our morning coffee.

When you combine that with the fact that so much of that media is impersonal and solicitous, sent by brands and not by humans, nonprofits have a huge opportunity to cut through the noise. So, what do stewardship communications at an ideally multi-channel nonprofit look like?

Assuming you've followed my segmentation advice earlier in the book, here is a sample multi-channel workflow for a new, online donor in the first few months of the relationship. Keep in mind, you can and should customize this advice, based on what you know about your donor community and the resources available to you.

Segment: First-time Donor, Online Gift

- automated email confirmation (immediately)
- personal email (within 1 hour), including a link to a video
- welcome packet by mail (within 3 days), including
  - form letter with handwritten signature
  - handwritten note
  - copy of the most recent print newsletter
- email newsletter (monthly)
- email update with impact story (quarterly)
- second gift ask (within 90 days of 1st gift)
- print newsletter (quarterly)
- handwritten thank-you note from board member (randomly)

Assuming this supporter is also following you on social media, you'll also gain those impressions.

Moving to and from digital and analog isn't the only way to nail a multi-channel campaign. It's possible to stay within the digital channel and still use multiple communication formats (e.g., email, social media, text, video, voicemail).

However, I cannot understate the impact that analog communications can have in our digital-saturated world. A handwritten note or a thank-you phone call will stand out because of its rarity and novelty. The impact I am suggesting could be "mantle or refrigerator worthy"—something donors could feel bad about throwing out right away.

One word of caution: Don't let your own preferences or stereotypes rule your decision-making. It's easy to say, "Older donors prefer mail" and "Millennials only want digital," or "I don't like getting texts (so no one does)," but you could be missing out on making an impact.

As a millennial, I can say that the only handwritten notes or thank-you voicemails I get are from nonprofits (the ones we've supported for years). Boomers that are the fastest growing segment of social media users. Don't make assumptions.

What about donor preference? It's a good thought. After all, you don't want to annoy donors. If a donor tells you not to mail them, or not to email them, you should absolutely honor that request.

However, do not go out of your way to solicit a channel preference. Many nonprofits ask their supporters, "How would you like to hear from us?" giving them a choice between mail, email, phone, or other channels.

Tom Ahern warns against the implications of this question:

But those questions have unspoken implications and generate answers that seem solid but could be as flimsy as balsa wood.

"Would you like more email?" "NO!"

"Would you like a piece of inspirational email every couple of weeks showing you exactly how wonderful your support has been to someone who depends on your compassion and kindness?" "Well, yeah, maybe."

Every channel has the potential to fall flat. Telemarketing solicitations are much different than a thank-you phone call from a board member, but both are in the phone channel. If your supporters are only getting phone solicitations, of course they are going to opt out of the channel! When seeking donor preference, make it your goal to ascertain interest and frequency preferences, as well as channel.

DonorVoice relates a story of a test run by the American Diabetes Association (ADA) in an acquisition piece. The association's control package had no ability to express a preference, but its test version allowed recipients to share their highest priorities, which included the following:

- finding a cure
- helping patients and families
- providing access to care for diabetes
- supporting medical professionals

This test version had a $3.40 increase in average gift size and a 11.6% increase in overall revenue.

Now, ADA has a basis for what *kind* of stories to tell, which is much more powerful than only knowing in which format to tell those stories. How they're delivered becomes almost irrelevant.

Don't be so quick to ditch a channel because you don't think it's providing return on investment. It's more likely that you have a content problem, not a delivery system problem. A multi-channel communications strategy works best when you're telling the right stories to the right audience at the right time—while surprising and delighting the recipient.

CHAPTER 34

Gamification

If you were walking up out of a subway station or a parking garage, what would it take to make you take the stairs instead of the escalator or the elevator?

Back in 2009, automaker Volkswagen wanted to promote a public health campaign, so they transformed staircases in public spaces into player pianos (like the one from the movie *Big* starring Tom Hanks). By transforming the staircase into a piano, they made the more strenuous option fun, and thus vastly increased the amount of people who chose the more health-conscious option.

Imagine if the mundane and arduous day-to-day tasks of a fundraiser could be transformed into something more fun and rewarding. One up-and-coming technology trend could make that happen.

What is Gamification?

Gamification is the marriage of gaming elements—like points, achievements, and progress meters—and everyday tasks. Tasks become less monotonous and more enjoyable when you are able to track your progress in real-time and compete with yourself and others.

It's likely that you've already experienced gamification, even if you weren't aware of it. An entire cottage industry exists around fitness, productivity, and efficiency apps. If you wear a Fitbit or an Apple Watch, you know how game elements can make a typically dreaded task (e.g., exercise) more entertaining. Apps like Mint.com keep your household budgeting in check, while Automatic allows you to track and improve your driving habits.

Many researchers, sociologists, and game designers have been studying how and why gamification is so effective in helping us maintain good habits. In her book *Reality Is Broken: Why Games Make Us Better and How They Can Change the World,* Jane McGonigal posits that gaming makes us more optimistic, builds up bonds of trust and cooperation, and gives "epic meaning" to our tasks. Check out her TED Talk for an excellent overview of the power of gamification.

Games, however, aren't just for entertainment anymore. They can be vital to helping us reach our goals. So, how will gamification change the nonprofit sector?

With limited funding sources, nonprofit success is dependent upon individual and institutional performance. Fundraisers track donation amounts, cost of acquisition, donor retention, and lifetime value. Communicators track media impressions, email open and click-through rates, website visits, and website conversions. Services staff track metrics like program attendance, physician referrals, and consultations, among many others.

Knowing where you are at all times is absolutely critical. Unfortunately, few tools are available that allow progress tracking in real-time, let alone in a manner that makes the pursuit of these metrics collaborative, competitive, fun, and rewarding.

This is what gamification can offer nonprofits.

Prediction: The tools you use on a daily basis will feature more and more gaming elements.

Imagine if your donor database rewarded you for reaching a new donor retention milestone, or your email provider scored your emails based on open and click-through rates. It won't be long until your tools feel more engaging and less utilitarian. What if data entry or moves management felt more like a game than a stodgy task? Would turnover decrease? Would more people in the organization use the software?

Prediction: Fundraisers will leverage technology to make fund-raising competitive, collaborative, and fun for the donor.

Some peer-to-peer and other third-party fundraising campaigns like Brackets for Good or Omaha Gives! are already taking advantage of game elements to help nonprofits raise money. But what if these game elements extended to all levels and modes of giving? Imagine your donor logging into a dashboard where they could see a history of their own gifts and compare their giving to others in their community. What if they could see, in real-time, the impact of their donations and be challenged to give more in order to unlock an achievement or help reach a collaborative campaign milestone?

The same could be said for volunteers. Imagine an app that tracks volunteerism in the same way a fitness app tracks calories burned and miles logged.

Prediction: Nonprofit organizations will build out services that feature gaming elements.

It isn't just the fundraisers who can have all the fun. In fact, there are already numerous examples of forward-thinking nonprofits that harness the power of gamification. Take, for example, a nonprofit like GameDesk that creates games to engage low-proficient K-12 students, or Nine13sports, an organization that promotes youth health and wellness by gamifying the traditional bike-riding experience.

After reading this section, you may become more aware of the game elements already present in your daily life. If you don't yet believe in the power of gamification, pick up a Fitbit or download an app like Habit RPG or Super Better. Not only will you be hooked, but your quality of life will improve in the process.

CHAPTER 35

Augmented Reality and Virtual Reality

A few years ago, you may remember crowds of people congregating in public spaces like parks, airports, and malls with their necks craned down toward their cell phones while playing Pokémon Go, an interactive mobile game where players can catch virtual Pokémon on their cell phones.

Pokémon Go wasn't the first, but it was arguably the most successful example of augmented reality, a technology that enables digital content to be projected onto or to interact with real-world environments. For example, you can hold up your cell phone on a city street and see reviews appear for all the restaurants within your camera frame. It's a big step up from the QR code, which allows your cell phone to follow a static image to a website URL.

Interestingly, many nonprofits capitalized on the Pokémon Go craze when it was at its height. The Indiana State Museum sent out a timely email encouraging visitors to play the game on museum grounds, while the Muncie Animal Shelter encouraged potential pet adopters to take dogs up for adoption on a walk while trying to catch Pokémon.

Augmented reality has a lot of practical uses for nonprofits beyond just facilitating the virtual captures of imaginary monsters. Direct mail pieces can become interactive, and events can become more immersive through this technology. It can also help facilitate empathy by allowing supporters to experience a nonprofit's services from the recipients' point of view. It can even be used on the programming side to help those service recipients directly.

Wild Apricot has a library of excellent and comprehensive case studies of several nonprofits using augmented reality. For example, a Dutch nonprofit called the Dolphin Swim Club uses underwater VR (virtual reality) goggles to allow people with disabilities to virtually swim with dolphins in their community pool as a form of therapy. An opera house created a video that allows people to experience *The Nutcracker* behind the scenes by watching dancers practicing, sets being built, or seeing what it's like backstage.

Imagine the possibilities for your nonprofit!

CHAPTER 36

Machine Learning and Artificial Intelligence

Even though I've been bearish on the amount of automation that our software—specifically our donor database and online giving programs—are capable of, I do predict that software sophistication will make possible things we can hardly imagine today.

Fundraising tools are already in development and just now hitting the market that are expected to quickly provide insights to nonprofits that would normally take hundreds of hours to find after pouring over data manually. Someday very soon, you can expect standard and affordable features in software that will alerts fundraisers when . . .

- a donor is about to lapse, and what you can do right now to prevent it
- a donor is ready for an upgrade request, and what amount to ask for

- a donor abandoned an online donation page, and how you should follow-up
- a donor passed away or changed email addresses or mailing addresses

On the donor side, not only will giving be virtually frictionless, but the experience will be custom-tailored and unique from any other donor's experience. Imagine online donation forms that auto-fill, update dynamically, and suggest gift amounts based on the donor's previous website activity, previous giving, geographic location, and other demographic information. Though online giving can be clunky now, it won't be long until the barrier to giving online is nearly non-existent.

Conversely, some tools may produce efficiencies while sacrificing the human touch. Automated letter writing services that use fonts mimicking human handwriting, chat bots, emerging social networks, point-of-sale donations (credit card swipers and dippers), and automatic letter mailing fulfillment (that prevents personalized, handwritten elements) will need to be considered shrewdly. Early adopters are sometimes rewarded, but as we've covered previously, every new technology comes with the danger of being abused or underutilized, so vet oncoming advancements responsibly.

CHAPTER 37

Favorite Tools, Vendors and Resources

One of the benefits of living in today's era of Silicon Valley startups is the multitude of affordable and powerful SaaS (software-as-a-service) products whose features were unavailable to all but the largest for-profit organizations due to price and complexity.

Here are a few of my favorite products that can give your nonprofit an edge, at little-to-no cost:

Unbounce

Unbounce is a great tool for creating beautiful and responsive landing pages. It's compatible with many of the leading website CMSs, including WordPress, and comes with tons of templates designed by conversion rate optimization experts.

HotJar

HotJar will analyze the activity of website visitors and generate heat maps that show what areas of each web page get the most attention. It's useful in optimizing your online donation pages and other conversion pages.

Google Optimize

If your online giving provider or website CMS does not allow for A/B testing, you can easily run tests through Google Optimize. Within the tool, you can create variations of live pages on your site and see which one performs better.

Canva

Canva is a free tool (with some premium upgrades available) that allows users to create beautiful and professional graphics, posters, and other images with little graphic design experience or knowledge.

Moz

Moz is essentially an SEO consultant in your pocket. After creating an account, it will monitor your website and give you easy-to-understand action items for optimizing your site.

Yoast

WordPress users can install the Yoast plugin and get many of the same benefits of a Moz subscription. It will connect your website to Google Analytics and Google Search Console, create and submit sitemaps, and suggest ideas for optimization of content like blog posts.

Vidyard

Vidyard is a browser plugin that connects to your webcam, allowing you to record and distribute personalized videos, as well as track when they've been viewed and opened.

Crystal

Crystal analyzes all of the information about a person online, like their LinkedIn profile, and gives you personalized, situation-specific advice to communicate effectively and write persuasively to them.

Mention

Mention is a monitoring tool that scours for web and social mentions and delivers them to you via email and through a web dashboard. You can even generate reports for brand activity over time. It's a nice solution for larger teams that field a high volume of mentions.

A marketing tech stack that includes these tools will put your communications in truly rarified air.

Conclusion

We've come a long way, and now it's time to wrap things up with some parting thoughts.

When traveling, I try to fly Southwest if I can. They have some of the clearest brand values of anyone in the airline industry, and it shows through everything they do. Plus, bags fly free.

On a recent flight, a Southwest flight attendant showed why their brand creates such loyal customers. While taxiing to the gate after landing, the attendant opened up the intercom and began singing "Nobody Does It Better," the old Carly Simon hit. She had a beautiful singing voice, and everyone on the plane seemed all at once amazed by what was happening.

Numerous cell phones started appearing over the tops of seats. Passengers were photographing and recording the performance! I overheard several say they were tweeting and Instagramming the footage. Many walked off the plane with a smile on their face.

If you weren't flying Southwest that day, you probably wouldn't have given the airline a thought. But if you saw your friends sharing that content, you'd be enjoying the experience with them. Not only was the song shared by passengers on social media free advertising and free publicity for Southwest but doing something so shareable also enhanced brand loyalty among the passengers.

Compare that to another flight I took on United. Actually, I honestly have no idea what airline it was. It might have been Delta. The point is that it wasn't Southwest. I know when I'm on a Southwest flight, and this was not a Southwest flight.

Something odd happened on this non-Southwest flight, and a fellow passenger let me know that it's a common occurrence on other airlines. Prior to descent, the flight attendant took to the intercom system to pitch us an airline credit card, promising a free quantity of frequent flier miles in exchange for signing up for the card. After the end of her sales pitch, another flight attendant walked up the entire length of the cabin holding up the applications, waving them in front of every row he passed.

Not a single person took an application. It was nearly midnight and many passengers were trying to nap.

How often is a new credit card account opened following a sales pitch by an airline's flight attendant? Probably, the flight attendants get enough applicants for the practice to be worth it, but at what cost? What about diminished brand perception and customer loyalty? Needless to say, no passengers on the plane got out their phones to record the sales pitch, let alone share it online.

When it comes to your nonprofit, do you strive to create a memorable experience and relationship with your donors, or do you simply go for the cold, hard sell? If there were fewer nonprofits that operated like the non-Southwest airline and more that operated like Southwest, the average donor retention rate would be much higher.

How can you create a memorable experience for your supporters, one that doesn't involve a solicitation? Maybe it's sharing valuable content, writing a handwritten thank-you note, or offering to take a first-time donor out for coffee to tell them what their support means for the organization. Something unexpected! Something memorable! What matters to your donor should matter to you.

There's no shortage of *shiny new things* that fundraisers need to worry about. And while nonprofits have been successful for hundreds of years without any of them, there are hundreds of bosses, board members, consultants, and vendors telling you that not paying attention to them will spell certain doom for your organization.

The result? Declining donor retention rates and increasing levels of staff burnout and turnover.

Wise nonprofit leaders will discern what could be useful and what ultimately will be a distraction. This is as much of a skill as implementing all the new tools and strategies out there.

Thanks for reading.

References

INTRODUCTION

Fundraising Effectiveness Project. 2005-2018. "Fundraising Effectiveness Survey" http://afpfep.org/reports/

Giving USA. "Giving USA Report" https://givingusa.org/

The Chronicle of Philanthropy. 2018. "The Disappearing Donor." June 5, 2018. https://www.philanthropy.com/specialreport/the-disappearing-donor/172

CHAPTER 1

Fundraising Effectiveness Project. 2005-2018. "Fundraising Effectiveness Survey." http://afpfep.org/reports/

Greenfeld, James M. 1999. *Fund Raising: Evaluating and Managing the Fund Development Process.* Wiley Publishing.

Panas, Jerry. 2018. "14 characteristics of planned giving donors." Jerold Panas, Linzy & Partners, Inc. October 22, 2018. https://panaslinzy.com/14-characteristics-of-planned-giving-donors/

CHAPTER 2

Adrian Sargeant. 2011. "Managing Donor Defection." Campbell Rinker. http://www.campbellrinker.com/Managing_donor_defection.pdf

Kevin Schulman. 2011. "Donor Commitment Report." September 20, 2011. https://agitator.thedonorvoice.com/national-donor-commitment-study-and-proof-of-link-between-donor-attitudes-and-behavior/

Jay, Elaine & Sargeant, Adrian. 2011. *Building Donor Loyalty: The Fundraiser's Guide to Increasing Lifetime Value.* Wiley Publishing.

Penelope Burk. "The 2018 Burk Donor Survey Report." Cygnus Research. https://cygresearch.com/product/the-2018-burk-donor-survey-report/

McConkey-Johnston International UK. http://mcconkey-johnston.com/

CHAPTER 4

Shattuck, Steven. Nonprofit Marketing Guide. 2014. "Nonprofits and Communication Segmenting." Bloomerang. April 22, 2014. https:// bloomerang.co/blog/infographic-nonprofits-and-communication-segmenting/

CHAPTER 5

Ashmore, Deb. 2019. "Trends in Sustainer Giving – Key Findings from the 2019 donorCentrics Sustainer Summit." NPEngage. April 19, 2019. https://npengage.com/nonprofit-fundraising/trends-in-sustainer-giving-2019/

Sargeant, Adrian. 2011. "Managing Donor Defection." Campbell Rinker. http://www.campbellrinker.com/Managing_donor_defection.pdf

Schulman, Kevin. 2011. "Donor Commitment Report." September 20, 2011. https://agitator.thedonorvoice.com/national-donor-commitment-study-and-proof-of-link-between-donor-attitudes-and-behavior/

Target Analytics. 2009. "DonorCentrics US Recurring Giving Benchmarking Analysis." https://www.blackbaud.com/files/resources/downloads/Research_RecurringGivingSummary_March2010.pdf

CHAPTER 7

U.S. Census Bureau. 2019. 2019 US Migration Report. https://www.northamerican.com/migration-map

PART III INTRO

The Blackbaud Institute for Philanthropic Impact. 2017. "Charitable Giving Report: How Nonprofit Fundraising Performed in 2017." https://institute.blackbaud.com/asset/2017-charitable-giving-report/

M+R. 2018. "The M+R 2018 Benchmark Study." April 25, 2018. https://www.mrss.com/lab/big-news-the-2018-mr-benchmarks-study-is-live-now/

CHAPTER 10

Ashmore, Deb. 2019. "Trends in Sustainer Giving – Key Findings from the 2019 donorCentrics https://npengage.com/nonprofit-fundraising/trends-in-sustainer-giving-2019/

Sustainer Summit." NPEngage. April 19, 2019.

MacLaughlin, Steve. 2017 "3 Truths and 1 Lie about Online Donors." Huffington Post. July 5, 2017. http://www.huffingtonpost.com/entry/3-truths-and-1-lie-about-online-donors_us_595cf48de4b0326c0a8d13fb

CHAPTER 12

Ashmore, Deb. 2019. "Trends in Sustainer Giving – Key Findings from the 2019 donorCentrics Sustainer Summit" NPEngage. April 19, 2019 https://npengage.com/nonprofit-fundraising/trends-in-sustainer-giving-2019/

CHAPTER 20

Bernstein, Daniel. 2015. "Email Marketing Chart: Personalized Subject Lines" MarketingSherpa. June 16, 2015. https. ://www.marketingsherpa.com/article/chart/personal-subject-lines

Mailchimp. "Personalizing Subject Lines: Does It Help or Hurt Open Rates." https://blog.mailchimp.com/personalizing-subject-lines-does-it-help-or-hurt-open-rates/

CHAPTER 23

Schulman, Kevin. 2011. "Donor Commitment Report." September 20, 2011. https://agitator.thedonorvoice.com/national-donor-commitment-study-and-proof-of-link-between-donor-attitudes-and-behavior/

PART V INTRO

Stratten, Scott. 2014. Brands: Stop Complaining About Facebook. January 17, 2014. https://www.youtube.com/watch?v=CznXMFXaUqQ

Muller, Derek. Veritasium, 2014. Facebook Fraud. https://www.youtube.com/watch?v=oVfHeWTKjag

CHAPTER 24

Rainie, Lee, Aaron Smith and Maeve Duggan. 2013. "Coming and Going on Facebook," Pew Research. Feb 5, 2013. https://www.pewresearch.org/internet/2013/02/05/coming-and-going-on-facebook/

Simone, Sonia. 2015. "Digital Sharecropping: The Most Dangerous Threat to Your Content Marketing Strategy," Copyblogger. July 28, 2015. https://copyblogger.com/digital-sharecropping/

CHAPTER 25

Mosseri, Adam. 2018. Bringing People Closer Together," Facebook. January 11, 2018. https://about.fb.com/news/2018/01/news-feed-fyi-bringing-people-closer-together/

CHAPTER 26

DonorVoice. 2011. "Donor Commitment Report." September 20, 2011. https://agitator.thedonorvoice.com/national-donor-commitment-study-and-proof-of-link-between-donor-attitudes-and-behavior/

CHAPTER 31

Schreifels, Jeff. 2015. "Serving Your Donors Means Asking." Veritus Group. October 21, 2015. https://veritusgroup.com/serving-your-donors-means-asking/

CHAPTER 33

Ellinger, Nick. Quote reported in "Feedback Week: Channel and Volume Preferences." February 14, 2018. https://agitator.thedonorvoice.com/feedback-week-channel-and-volume-preferences/

Network for Good. 2018. "Our Digital Dilemma." Network for Good. https://learn.networkforgood.com/white-paper-our-digital-dilemma-website.html

Ellinger, Nick. 2018. "TEST RESULTS: You Raise More Money When You Listen to Donors' Preferences," DonorVoice. August 23, 2018. http://agitator.thedonorvoice.com/listen-to-donors-preferences-get-more-donors-money/

CHAPTER 34

Volkswagen. "The Fun Theory." Volkswagen. October 26, 2009. https://www.youtube.com/watch?v=SByymar3bds

McGonigal, Jane. 2010. *Reality Is Broken: Why Games Make Us Better and How They Can Change the World*, Penguin Books.

CHAPTER 35

Ibele, Terry. 2018. "The Nonprofit's Guide to Augmented Reality." Wild Apricot. January 8, 2018. https://www.wildapricot.com/blogs/newsblog/2018/01/08/augmented-reality-nonprofit

Made in the USA
Columbia, SC
21 November 2021

49429021R00137